"In this entertaining and often moving book, DeMasco takes a gritty and unapologetic look at the difficulties of growing up in modern society, and offers lessons from his own life and the wisdom of the Shaolin monks . . . a well-crafted perspective into how ancient teachings can be applied to modern problems."
—*Publishers Weekly*

"DeMasco's book is unique. . . . Self-proven methods on avoiding negativity, anger, and victimization, all told with frank, simple language—that's a nice change from the condescending pomp of some other self-improvement books."
—*Salt Lake City Tribune*

"Thanks for taking good care of us. What you do is important. Keep up the good work."   —"Marvelous" Marvin Hagler, former World Middleweight Champion

"Thank you for giving so much to our nation's children."
—Richard W. Riley, former U.S. Secretary of Education

"*The Shaolin Way* is a beautiful book. It was a gift to me as I am sure it will be to others who read it. Congratulations."
—Cheryl Angelheart, publisher, *Black Belt* magazine

"I commend your dedication to improving the lives of our younger generation."   —U.S. representative Rosa DeLauro, Anti-Crime Youth Council

"Steve DeMasco has an incredible story to tell. This great student of life has become a master at making a profound difference in the lives of others."   —Michael Bolton, singer and activist

About the Author

STEVE DEMASCO is a tenth-degree black belt in Shaolin kung fu who has dedicated his life to helping prisoners, teenagers, abused women, and many others who have lost their way. He lectures around the world on behavior modification and reducing school violence. He lives in New Hampshire with his wife and three sons.

THE SHAOLIN WAY

少
林

THE SHAOLIN WAY

10 Modern Secrets of Survival from a Shaolin Kung Fu Grandmaster

Steve DeMasco

with Alli Joseph

HARPER

NEW YORK • LONDON • TORONTO • SYDNEY

HARPER

A hardcover edition of this book was published in 2005 by HarperEntertainment, an imprint of HarperCollins Publishers.

HarperCollins books may be purchased for educational, business, or sales promotional use. For information please write: Special Markets Department, HarperCollins Publishers, 10 East 53rd Street, New York, NY 10022.

FIRST HARPER PAPERBACK PUBLISHED 2006.

Designed by Jeffrey Pennington

Library of Congress Cataloging-in-Publication Data has been applied for.

ISBN 0-06-057456-9
ISBN-10: 0-06-057457-7 (pbk.)
ISBN-13: 978-0-06-057457-4 (pbk.)

06 07 08 09 10 ❖/RRD 10 9 8 7 6 5 4 3 2 1

To the people who have majorly influenced my life, in the order in which they came into my life.

My Mom, Carol G. DeMasco, the true Shaolin Disciple.

Vinny Vecchionne, my boxing trainer, mentor, and the person who kept me in school.

Paul Newman, the most generous, kind, and inspirational person I have ever met.

President William J. Clinton, for all your faith and encouragement, and for making me feel that I was important to you and our country.

Barry Mawn, one of the true heroes of 9/11. Thank you for your friendship and allowing me to be part of the greatest law enforcement agency in the world, the Federal Bureau of Investigation.

My wife, Kelly; and my boys, Michael, Nicco, and Gianni— my inspiration for the rest of my life!

It will all be okay in the end.
If it's not okay,
it's not the end.

—Anonymous

CONTENTS

CONTENTS

FOREWORD

The Shaolin Temple is one of the most popular and far-spreading manifestations of China's traditional Buddhist culture. It has become an integral part of human spiritual civilization, to be accepted and respected by people of different cultures around the world. Shaolin kung fu has had the same influence on people of different cultures. It is a bridge of mutual understanding, contributing to the advancement of human peace and friendship.

Steve DeMasco has respected Buddhism and loved Shaolin kung fu since childhood. He established his United Studios of Self-Defense to gather new Shaolin followers, as well as teach Shaolin kung fu. He has been very generous and ready to help the poor and homeless children to receive schooling education for free with his limited savings. This is a mercy and benevolence which is advocated by Buddhism.

Since he was accepted as a disciple of the Shaolin Temple,

Steve DeMasco has led hundreds of USSD students to visit the Ancestral court for pilgrimage tours, and donated his time to help the ongoing Renovation Project of the Shaolin Temple.

I believe that with the publication of this book, more American friends will have a better understanding of traditional Chinese culture, and further understanding of the Shaolin spirit. For sure it will purify people's souls.

Abbott Shi Yongxin
China Songshang Shaolin Temple
Buddhist year of 2548

INTRODUCTION

THE MYTH OF THE MOUNTAIN

You could say I didn't have the best start in life. I was born in 1953 to Concetta and Al DeMasco in Spanish Harlem, where I lived until I was nine. My mother, who for some reason was always called "Carol," had two wooden legs and four fingers on one hand, both resulting from birth defects and abuse by her unhappy mother. Carol was my inspiration and my reason for living until she died several years ago. My father, Al, was a psychotic, abusive man who beat and sexually abused me repeatedly as a child, until my mother remarried in 1962 and moved us away to Brockton, Massachusetts. Al disappeared from my life when I was sixteen.

Coming from a really bad beginning like this—where I was lucky not to become a poverty statistic in the ghetto—there were a lot of changes I needed to make on my journey over the years. About thirty-five years ago, when I first learned about Shaolin philosophy and the kung fu martial arts that go with it, I had no idea how it would profoundly change my life, but it did. It was Shaolin—a mysterious practice created by a special group of men fifteen hundred years ago in China—that saved me.

These men believed that to have total balance in life, one must be fulfilled spiritually and physically, and find a balance between aggression and peace. This balance came by practicing equal parts kung fu martial arts, natural healing, compassionate actions in the world outside their temple walls, and intense study of Buddhism. They spent their lives unraveling the roots of life challenges that all humans still struggle with today, regardless of race or socioeconomic background. These men were the fighting Shaolin monks, and their tradition still lives.

WHAT IS SHAOLIN?

Many people believe that most modern martial arts are descended from Shaolin (which means "small forest" in Chinese). The original Shaolin temple was built in northern China (Hunan Province) by the emperor just for religious study around the fourth century CE (common era), and was burned down by warring emperors in the eighteenth century. After it was burned down, rebuilt, and then trashed again, a remaining piece of the last temple was turned into the current temple near Deng Feng, China.

Scholars write that the kung fu element of

Shaolin began about a thousand years after the
original Buddha lived, when Bodhidharma
(known as "Ta Mo" in Chinese and "Daruma" in
Japanese—*bodhi* means "enlightened mind,"
dharma is Sanskrit for "law" or "teaching"), a
Buddhist monk and prince from India, came to
teach the Shaolin monks a nonlethal form of self-
defense in the sixth century CE. As monks, they
had taken vows of peace, and so could not kill
when attacked, which happened a lot during
those challenging and violent times of ruling-
class upheaval. Shaolin kung fu became a sort of
"meditation in motion," which protected them
from invaders while still allowing them to stay
true to their vows. With these new skills, they became the fighting Shaolin monks.

Shaolin revolves around the Chan Buddhist religion, a particular blend of Buddhism with Con-
fucianism and Taoism (also known as Daoism),
and relies on an understanding of what it means
to be a fighter and a warrior. The fighting
Shaolin monks were thought to have the most famous and most advanced kung fu methods in all
of Asia, even though a lot of the time they weren't
fighting. Shaolin works backward: You study to
be able to kill, but you can't be effective unless you
learn that violence should never be used unless
you're protecting someone else's life.

Today there are thousands of Buddhist monks all over China. They all look very similar to each other, with their simple robes and shaved heads. But while they may all dress the same and look the same, there is only one remaining Shaolin temple near Deng Feng, and its inhabitants are a small group of men—there are about *fifty* of them, out of about a billion people in China. These men have special skills that I spent thirty-five years trying to learn, and then sharing with my students: juvenile offenders, convicted murderers, abused women, stay-at-home moms, frustrated teenagers, and successful businesspeople alike.

Now I want to share them with you.

EVERYDAY FIGHTS

In more than thirty years of working with men, women, children, and families as a behaviorist, I have seen and done a lot of fighting. We are all fighting in one way or another: we're fighting to survive every day of our lives. We fight to wake up some mornings when the day looks like crap outside, and we fight to feel good when we're miserable and depressed. I call this kind of fighting "mental warfare" because we're using our heads to fight the intangibles in life: depression, egotism, hatred, anger, greed, selfishness, and just about every negative tendency, emotion, or action that makes us dissatisfied with our lives and hurts us deeply, sometimes in ways we don't even recognize.

I spent many years as a kid fighting in the streets to protect myself from bullies without knowing how, then fighting with skill as a boxer, then learning a whole different way of fighting through Shaolin kung fu—and that's a lot of fighting. But the monks did more than just fight for a purse or for fun: they fought with the goal of ridding the world of misery, learning to protect themselves so they could then protect and help other people. All Buddhist religions preach that same goal, but the Shaolin monks were different because they were warriors. And so are we.

When I talk to kids or adults who are struggling with personal problems or situations, and we hit a roadblock because they don't believe the lessons I'm trying to teach them about how Shaolin can help them change their lives, I always say the same thing: "How do you feel?"

"I feel like shit," most respond.

"Think about this," I say. "What you have been doing up to this point obviously hasn't worked for you, or you would not be where you are. Unless you have an alternative plan, then you have *nothing to lose and everything to gain*. I know how you feel: I have been in the same place many times in my life, and each and every time these lessons have worked for me. If you follow the path and don't go off of it, I guarantee it will work for you."

THE THREE TREASURES OF SHAOLIN

The Shaolin monks live by three main principles, called the "Three Treasures."

CHAN is the heart of kung fu. It means constantly being cued in to the present, or the "here and now." Chan suggests practicality by living life in the present, and the need to look at issues or situations from all angles, rather than your own personal frame of reference.

HEALTH, meaning both internal and external health, deals with keeping the body in good working order and living in harmony with its needs. Medicinal and *qigong* ("internal energy") practice are used to heal the body and maintain proper internal organ function alongside the muscles and bones. "Forms" (dancelike movements that imitate animal movements and behavior), from the movements themselves, to the external strengthening of the body, to internal conditioning of the organs, combine with medicine and energy work to create health.

SELF-DEFENSE. The monks believe that the body must be kept in balance at all times, and so they use self-defense training as well as fighting scenarios to delve into their personal demons and attachments, and to root out what they believe are the sources of all ignorance: fear and greed.

A SURVIVAL GUIDE

This book offers a kind of blueprint for survival: a guide for life based on Shaolin philosophy that can help you change your own. The Shaolin monks have a whole different set of rules for living than anybody else, and these were created for a reason. Before they became fighting monks, they had many of the same problems as the rest of us. Their health was bad, they were out of shape, they couldn't focus on their religion, they were depressed, and they wanted to be loved. In short, sometimes their lives sucked too.

In order to stop feeling bad, the monks decided to do a few things differently. They began to follow a course of action every day that would *create change within them so they could effect change in the world outside* their temple walls, ridding it of misery. This reflects one of the central ideas in Buddhism, which suggests that the only way to improve your own life is to help someone else, because we are all essentially the same.

When Bodhidharma came down off that mountain and said he'd teach them to fight, they thought they would learn how to fight their enemies and get in better shape right away, but they didn't. First they had to learn more about Buddhist law from their masters at the temple, as well as many survival skills like healing using wild herbs and how to eat off the land. Later they learned to practice the elite fighting Shaolin kung fu forms that made them famous. Finally, well prepared for whatever came into their paths mentally or physically, the monks were sent on spiritual journeys out into the world, where they had to apply what they had learned in their small setting.

TRAVELING THROUGH OURSELVES

So how can Shaolin provide the tools to help you change *your* life? Why is it different from any other method? Right off the bat, you may think that fighting is a big part of the lessons contained in this book, since Shaolin is tied to the martial arts. This is not true. Where the fighting Shaolin monks used fighting techniques to keep themselves fit and focused, we are going to use our own everyday situations, because unlike the monks, we have a lot more to deal with in everyday life than waking up, eating, praying, and practicing. We have to deal with reality on its most manic scale—like heading off to work, being in a relationship, overcoming issues from the past, and much, much more.

The skills we need to function today may be different from those the monks practiced so many years ago in the temple and on their journeys, but the principles Shaolin taught them are still the same: to really live your life every day and not just "get by" means dealing with change and breaking some of your "personal rules," two of the most difficult things for a person to do. Personal rules are behaviors you have been conditioned to have that keep you in negative patterns and create unhappiness. They are addictions, just like drinking and drugs, and they need to be broken.

Shaolin *will* give you all the tools to fight for a better version of your current life, but what it really teaches you is the way to true inner power. It shows you how to "fight" for your life and deal with your opponents without doing damage to others—whether they are your parents, enemies, or bullies, or even yourself. But the first and greatest battle is with ourselves.

With Shaolin, looking at the different kinds of "fights" you have each and every day can end up teaching you a lot about yourself. The catch is that you have to be ready to learn it—or it won't make a difference at all. Shaolin, like any other philosophy, can't help you if you don't engage: but it will always point the way.

The Monks and Us

What is the way? The monks' approach to finding a path toward happiness is quite different from ours in the West. They live by a set of rules set out by Buddhist law, a sort of "Ten Commandments," much as you find in Judaism and Christianity.

The monks choose to live a life of asceticism—one that has no use for material things. The things they consider on a daily basis may seem "limited" to us because they are generally concerned only with whether they have had enough to eat, are sick, and how they pray to Buddha and understand his teachings.

We believe *we* have a lot more to deal with every day. After all my years of attempting to understand the meaning of life, I feel great compassion for us. We have it really tough: we think we need to be perfect, and the ways in which we choose to pursue perfection are varied and complex.

You may think it's a lot easier to walk around in a temple all day with a shaved head, praying and doing kung fu, and that the monks focus on being "perfect" in a way that we cannot, because they are in a controlled environment. Our environment is much different: we live between freeways and free will, so we have to make some choices and some changes in our lives and acknowledge the myth of perfection; otherwise we'll always be unhappy and unfulfilled.

The desire to achieve perfection comes from a basic set of principles or "rules" that were laid out for us early in our lives. But, they don't work, no matter what our religion—Buddhism, Christianity, Islam, Judaism, or any other. I believe that we start out depressed in life because what most religions, and then our parents, teach us is that we have to live up to all of these commandments and expectations of perfection.

Point-blank, that's impossible.

By trying to be perfect, you could say that we're starting at the bottom of the barrel automatically. So it's no wonder that we live in guilt about how we live, and what we do each day for our entire lives, not knowing whether we are taking the right steps toward happiness. As humans trying to function in the world today, we are *totally* conflicted from the beginning, so naturally we're confused and we *can't* see a good path for ourselves.

Internal conflict manifests itself differently for everyone. Where you are in your life dictates what you feel. For a woman who got married very young and now has children and responsibility, inner conflict might mean feeling anxious about having missed out on much of her young life. While her friends were out drinking at bars and meeting guys, she was home with a newborn. The feeling that something has been missed out on brings sadness and conflict. Or if you're stuck in a job that you hate, but feel you need to be there because of your financial responsibilities, you are in conflict. If you're in your last year of high school and you want to drive an eighteen-wheeler for a living but your parents are both college professors and you know they will be devastated if you don't go to college, you're tormented inside.

Now, depending on your conscious and personal feelings of commitment to the things that are causing the conflict, you may be haunted each day, because these things represent the missing pieces of the "perfect person" you feel you will never become, or don't want to become.

Most religions have some things in common when it comes to the notion of achieving perfection, taking the wrong path, and being punished for it. The Bible, for one, teaches us that we were born from original sin—the Adam and Eve story, of course. "What the hell was that all about?" I've often asked, because following a philosophy that teaches us that we are essentially bad has always made me wonder—even as an observant Catholic (who has learned many things from Buddhism)—Where can you go from there?

As with the biblical commandments, the strict Buddhist law is impossible to follow exactly in everyday life, so over the centuries Buddhists developed a road map. These are a set of principles, or *other* rules, called the Ten Perfections, like having courage, pursuing truth, having a sense of duty and serenity, and being a giving person—all of which were designed to help them be happier, in spite of the impossibility of reaching perfection in their lives.

It is ironic that the very set of guidelines intended to help Buddhist monks get through their lives without being frustrated by the need to be perfect is called the "Perfections." Unlike the monks, we don't have our own "Perfections"; we simply strive to be perfect in our world, and because of this, we sometimes feel as if we're looking at a series of mountains we have to climb in order to get to the top of our form—to be the best at our jobs, the smartest, the richest, or the wisest people around.

But what Shaolin teaches, and what has evaded most of us, is that the mountain—whatever it means to you or me on any given day (a fight with your spouse, having to discipline your kids, losing money, feeling too tired to work out, writing a book, dealing with old demons)—is simply what you make it. In our haste to live our lives and get ahead, or be "perfect," we miss the point of the journey, and often blame circumstance for how our lives turn out. This mountain is one I just can't get past, we might think in despair.

The mountain—whatever it is—is a myth. The mightiest of things we must overcome are those that we erect in our own paths. Until we see that there is actually no mountain (or no obstacles to anything we want to accomplish) except the roadblocks we put in our own way, we will never go free.

This means going on a journey like the monks did hundreds of years ago, except this one is our own. They went to rid the world of misery; we go to rid *ourselves* of misery as a beginning. Each of us has to have his or her own kind of vision quest. The day you wake up and realize that you can create greater happiness for yourself and the people around you through a new way of living and surviving, your journey begins.

Focusing on the Journey

In the temple system, there is a tale about an exercise called "grabbing the pebble." A master will hold out his hand to a disciple, and on the palm rests a pebble. He will tell the disciple to snatch the pebble, but it is very hard to do, because the master has much more focus and training, and until he is as focused on getting the pebble as the master is on closing his hand, the disciple won't be able to grab it.

This idea is simple: If you're too quick to reach for something without proper focus, you usually miss it. Focus, from a Shaolin perspective, is the key to achieving anything important in our lives. Before I discovered Shaolin, I grabbed too fast for everything, had no focus, and didn't realize that I needed to look at *how* I was fighting for my life. For many years, I tried to snatch the pebble from whoever or whatever held it out to me, whether it was a job, a woman, more money, a friendship. I was focused on getting everything the pebble represented, not paying attention to how I could become mentally and physically quick enough to get the pebble out of the hand of life.

This kind of focus takes years to develop. Even in the physical fighting of Shaolin kung fu, you can't just punch or kick—you've got to think. After a while, you don't just think—you feel. And when you get really good, you don't just feel—you anticipate. And then you see that Shaolin is not simply about the fight—it's about the journey.

STRIDING TOWARD HAPPINESS

Lao Tzu, an ancient Chinese scholar, wrote, "The journey of a thousand miles begins with one step." Starting at the beginning of a new journey, this book will guide you as you take the road of your life's twists and turns, moment by moment, and learn to anticipate and solve problems like a Shaolin warrior monk. First you look down the road in frustration, seeing great mountains in the distance that you know you will have to cross.

Remember to take the journey step by step, moment by moment. There are no shortcuts. Throughout life, each and every encounter must be dealt with, and skipping over any one of them will only frustrate you and cause you more anxiety. The only way to move forward and change is to decide to "be where you are," taking conscious steps through different turns in the road of life—like feeling what it means to have focus and discipline. These are the building blocks of change, another concept this book addresses. Change happens every day, all around us, and accepting the inevitability of and need for it will enable you to examine your sense of self-worth, take responsibility for your actions in a new way, and become stronger inside.

As the road you're reading about bends, so will your own, and your anger should become balanced by what I offer you about compassion. This balance ("yin and yang," or equal forces of strength and weakness in the universe balancing each other) will lead you into a new and compassionate understanding of yourself, other people, power, and your own sense of structure and foundation in the world.

At the end of your journey, you—like the Shaolin monk—will hopefully find that you are able to accept your life and where you are, for better or worse, because you believe in yourself and your path, whatever it is. You'll also be surprised to see that there are no real mountains in your way after all.

The lessons I offer—a combination of Eastern philosophy and practical thinking I've learned the hard way—may seem to overlap at times, but this is because in life as in Buddhism, everything is connected. As you'll read later, I don't believe that any one action or behavior we take/do in our lives is unconnected to other ones, so it is in the spirit and recognition of this universal kick in the pants that I suggest you take in the information.

So, this book is about facing the challenges of a demanding life in a world that seems to insist on perfection and adaptation. It's also about a guy's journey working with thousands of people to change their lives, and in the process discovering he had made positive changes in his own.

This is not a book about *how* to live your life, but instead how to survive every day in ways more likely to bring happiness and inner peace. If you feel like a fighter every day, it can help you strengthen your life skills so that you're fighting for change and growth, and not just going in circles. Again, fighting—specifically, fighting to survive—is just the beginning, because true strength is about going out and helping someone else change his or her life, and discovering that this is the only way you can change your own life. It might seem counterintuitive now, but it won't after you read this book. You are about to go on a great journey. Walk with me.

THE SHAOLIN WAY

SURVIVAL IS NOT ENOUGH

Warfare is the greatest affair of state,
the basis of life and death,
the way (Tao) to survival or extinction;
it must be thoroughly pondered and analyzed.

—SUN TZU

Sun-Tzu said that the basis of life and death is whether one survives or dies. The idea that people get up every day to survive is a habit-forming concept, but we need to rely on it because getting up every day is a necessity of life. Therefore, it's an extremely difficult habit to get away from.

Most of the people in my world were survivors; they grew up in the projects, often went hungry, and didn't have clothes or shoes for school, and many had abusive or drug-addicted parents. It wasn't until much later in my life that I realized there are different levels of survival for all people, and that those levels depend on where we are in our lives. For children, young adults, or adults, survival can mean dealing with what I had to as a kid, or it can be something entirely different, like going to a job that many days you hate, dealing with the everyday pressures of life like bills, family issues, and education, and then just waiting for Friday to come to have the weekend. A lot of people spend the weekend just trying to get done what they couldn't do Monday through Friday, and then it starts all over.

Whether you're a monk or a regular guy, the quest for survival is a natural dynamic of life. In prehistoric times, a cave person's life was probably about staying away from hungry animals, natural disasters, and sickness. We have also been surrounded by war—something else we must survive—in some fashion for all time, in every part of the world. What we have not personally seen, we studied in school; when you cracked your history textbooks as a kid, what did you learn about? The Civil War. The War of 1812. World Wars I and II.

For many years I defined survival by my own experiences. However, I learned one very important fact about survival: It is not a condition only of the poor. It does not discriminate and does not care about your color, nationality, or socioeconomic status. The struggle to survive—just to get by—affects everyone, and can often feel like it's taking over our entire lives.

ARE YOU LIVING TO LIVE OR LIVING TO DIE?

We essentially have a choice about whether we want to live to live (enjoy life as we should be doing) or live to die (live to survive only). Humans were never really taught just to live to live. Society tells us that if we don't protect what we have, it will be taken away from us. Money and power in today's world are what a piece of fresh meat might have been to cave people; you have to grab on fiercely to what you find, catch, or earn, and fight everyone, including yourself, to keep it.

Therefore, the way you were trained to survive determines the methods you will *use* to survive. When we are born, our parents protect us. When we've learned to walk and talk, and have mastered a kind of day-to-day existence, we get thrown out of the house into something called "school." When we first get there, we don't know anyone or feel comfortable. Those whom we love have made us leave our home to go hang out with strangers, and we are introduced for the first time to people whom we will see more than we see our parents, who will have a profound effect on us for many years, and who will be essential to our self-worth, good or bad: our teachers.

At such a young age, none of us have the skills to master this new experience, so we come home with glue in our hair and a bruise where one of the other kids (also scared and uncomfortable in his or her new forced environment) hit us, and ask, "Why do I have to go to school? I want to stay home and be with you, Mom."

Here is where the fight for survival begins for most people. The answer from Mom comes: "Stevie, you have to go to school to get educated." The kindergartner or preschooler then asks, "What does that mean, Mom?" She probably told you that it means you'll go to school, get smarter, and then be able to get into a good college—all so you can get even smarter than that, and when you're big like Mommy and Daddy, you can have a good job and make a lot of money. It all starts here!

One of the major problems with learning to survive is that many of us spent so much of our young and adult life learning how to survive that there was little or no training on how to live—that is, balance it all so that we could survive and at the same time enjoy life.

I lived in the thoughtless "survival" mode for a long time,

without really "living." I worked six days a week, and on the seventh day I was on the phones and going to business functions that I would bring my family to, thinking that was good because I was spending time with them, even though sometimes they would be left standing around while I networked. I thought I was having a great life, but really, I was just surviving. What was my life really all about? Work, work, and more work. And when I'd go home and my wife or kids would need my help, I would get upset because hey, didn't they know how hard I worked—for all of us? When I use the term "living to die," it's because I wasn't living at all. I was working toward a goal that didn't include the very people in my life I love and care about. They were getting pushed to the side. I'd been surviving for so long on my own that I didn't know how to change my survival habits to include the people who were most important in my life.

The ties we make in this life don't go away. The decisions we make stick. The people we love continue to love us back. What we do in this life reverberates like a ripple in a pond, to everyone and everything around us. Therefore, it's essential that you ask yourself, What really matters, and why?

What I didn't realize at the time was that the effort we put into our friends and loved ones is far more valuable than the money we make. Money comes and goes, so at some point we have to ask ourselves, Whom are we actually being workaholics for, and why? How are we surviving? Are we spending each day "living," meaning enjoying the time we have here on this planet, or are we just working ourselves to death at the expense of everything around us—our families and friends—because we think it will give us something we never had, or because we're running away from a past we don't want to go back to?

THE 80/20 TECHNIQUE

There is something that I call the "80/20 Technique": it is an understanding that 80 percent of the time life can and should be good, and 20 percent of the time life will probably suck, because let's face it—you can't control everything.

Buddhists believe that bad things that happen in life (death, bad health, family problems, natural disasters, and more) are natural dynamics of everyday existence, and that as such they are going to happen no matter how hard we try to avoid them, or how good a person we try to be. The 80/20 Technique is just another way of accepting the fact that shit happens, and that when it does, not personalizing the pain that comes from the bad things (thinking "It's my fault" or "If only I had done X differently") makes it easier to deal with painful situations with a minimal amount of suffering.

I believe that one of the major reasons we as people have such a difficult time dealing with pain, disappointment—again, the natural dynamics of life—is how we are conditioned in this country by the "reward system."

As young children, many times we are rewarded for taking our first step, having good behavior, completing tasks independently—even saying "Mommy" or "Daddy" for the first time. Sometimes we're rewarded for playing sports well, getting good grades, cleaning our rooms, and many other things that we do reasonably well. As adults, we get rewarded for our work on the job, or being a good sports team coach for our kids, and everything in between, and sometimes it feels like complete overkill. In other parts of the world and especially for Shaolin warrior monks, much of what we're rewarded for in the West is *expected behavior*. That is, it is *expected* that a person will walk, clean his or her room, get good grades, play well at sports, do an outstanding job at work, and so on.

If we come to know that getting A's in school will be rewarded by our parents, and they will give us presents or money, or that cleaning our room and doing chores will get us a special dinner or praise or an allowance, then when we don't get these things later in life for doing everyday *expected* things, we are pissed off or disappointed.

Behaving well shouldn't mean a child is going to get a toy or something special for doing the *right thing*. Doing a good job at work as an adult shouldn't necessarily warrant a raise or an "employee of the month" award, or a special parking space for your car. We get rewarded so often in this country for all that we do right, that when bad things happen we really have *nowhere to go but down*.

If we did many positive things in life simply because they represented what we *should* do, and not because we expected to get something else out of the actions, we would get more perspective on what's real and what's not. If you're consistently given accolades at work because you're great at sales, what happens when one day everyone that normally gives you accolades is busy doing other things. Let's say you made the biggest sale ever; you would probably expect the biggest raise ever. But when you don't get it, you get depressed— what did I do wrong, why isn't anyone calling me, oh no, what if I get fired? These thoughts aren't based in reality, but if most of your life is based on a reward system, it's going to be that much more difficult to handle.

The 80/20 Technique can help by giving us some much-needed perspective. If we can accept that at least 20 percent of the time things are not going to go our way (for whatever reason—a natural disaster, a death, bad health, financial problems, etc.), it will free us up to deal with the difficulties and tragedies of life on our own. We'll be living to live instead of living for other people (in this example), which is the same as living to die, because when we live for things that are out of our control, instead of living for the moment, we aren't living at all.

THE JOYOUS LIFE

One would think that what it means to enjoy life would be easy to define. I can't tell you how many people I have asked to try, however, and instead of answering quickly, they really had to think. They didn't know. They didn't have any idea what enjoying life was. Many would say, "I'd like to win the lottery."

That's a nice thought; however, I have learned many things about money: I have had it, and I haven't had it. I don't have to tell you that I like my life better when I have money. Money gives people freedom: the freedom to travel, buy what they want, and do the things in life that hopefully give them joy. Still, I also know many people who have money and haven't the slightest idea how to live outside of "survival mode." They have spent so much time learning to "make it," then working to "keep it," that they have never learned how to live *with* it. To me, having money or not, "making it" means feeling good when you want to and *being with the people you love*.

I have almost gone bankrupt three times. Each and every time, I rebuilt my wealth to resume and protect my lifestyle and ego—again, the Westerner's idea of living well, which is an Easterner's nightmare because conducting your daily routine to acquire more money or power is his or her idea of living to die. But what good sense would motivate me to keep picking up the pieces and starting over again?

I started to think about it one day when I wondered why my mother, who was my greatest mentor, and I were so different. How could a woman with so many physical handicaps, two bad husbands, and another son who died of AIDS at thirty-two always seem to have a positive outlook on life?

I have studied my mother's behavior my whole life, and for a long time, the more educated in the ways of Shaolin and psychology I got, the more questions I had. My mom could truly have been a Shaolin warrior Buddhist monk. She had it so much worse than I or most other people, yet she was, for the most part, happy. On the other hand, I was always sad, lonely, and hurt. I often felt guilty for feeling this way, because my mom was such a pillar, and I wasn't.

My mother didn't have much: she didn't care about a lifestyle. All she cared about was her children, and helping others to improve the quality of their lives. I tried just caring about my kids and other people, only I still wasn't happy. There was something missing and I didn't even know it. My definition of survival was that my life sucked and that's the way it was.

I worked overtime to convince myself that I was happy: I made money, looked at where I came from, and what I had in comparison to that, as well as at the lives that I had affected in a positive way. This was all great, but the fact that I was still unhappy showed me something was very wrong. A couple of my close friends, who knew me better than most, would always say, "Steve, you have accomplished so much in your life, when are you going to start enjoying it?" I had a theory for that, too. I lived by the sword; that is, I was only as good as my last conquest, what I did yesterday was history, and what I was doing today was the one thing that counted.

This was a very unhealthy way of approaching my life. I wasn't getting any happier, and I never felt like I was really moving. That's because when you live by the sword—thinking that you're only as good as your last conquest—you're not living in the moment, or in reality. It doesn't take into account how much you've accomplished throughout your life, all the growth you've done, all the changes you've made, and without that warehouse of information behind you, as a kind of support system and meter for how far you've come, you're basically just setting yourself up for disaster.

The way I operated at that time is *great* if you want to spend the rest of your life in conquest mode, and kill yourself with a heart attack. You see, I was so consumed by my past and so afraid of having to go back to where I came from that I never learned how to live just to *live*. I never learned that over the years I'd developed some solid footing underneath me, and I could never go back to who I was in the past, even if I wanted to. But mentally—in my head—I hadn't realized this yet. Instead, I was so concerned with having enough, judging myself by how people viewed me, and getting people to like and approve of me that I was missing all that was around me.

Out of the mouth of the great Bruce Lee came the idea that you should not concentrate only on "the finger," or you will miss the rest of the hand. I was like a kid with attention deficit disorder: I focused on everything around me and missed what was right in front of me, *happiness*. As a result, I missed *everything*. I took on any project that excited or stimulated me, not taking into account the time it would take to complete it, and what I would be neglecting. I didn't turn anyone down, and I paid for it with lackluster career results, the disapproval of my wife, and the disappointment of my boys.

While living this kind of life, it was difficult for me to understand how a monk could be really happy. His entire life was focused around religion, kung fu training, and improving the quality of life for others. As most human beings do—and this is in the psychology books—I made excuses for the monks' happiness. It's easy for them, I thought. They have no responsibilities, no car payments, and no kids to take care of. Their food and living quarters are all provided for them.

Again, I missed what was right in front of me. I took out of the monks' existence what I defined as good for me and discarded the rest: you could use the kung fu to make your body and mind stronger, but that was where it ended for me. What I really missed was how to be happy and have peace of mind. I defined my happiness solely as having a strong mind and strong body, not realizing that being happy meant not only having the innate ability to survive, as I did when I was a kid, but training the mind to be at peace whether I had a lot of money or not.

But I preached the philosophy; I trained hard in kung fu (which is most likely the only thing that kept me from having a heart attack). Using it got me to a higher level, because when I crashed as usual after taking on too much, I would mentally take responsibility for it and ask myself why I had gotten to "this place" again. The answer was always the same. I was insecure, I wanted approval, I didn't realize that I couldn't control everything in the world, and I never looked back to all the things I'd accomplished to help give me footing when things were at their worst.

GROWING OUT OF SURVIVING AND INTO LIVING

When I was about fifteen, I got my ass kicked in one of the rough neighborhoods of Brockton, where I lived with my mother, sisters, and alcoholic stepfather, Mitch. The beatdown was pretty bad, I looked like hell, and I had to take myself to the hospital: I was afraid to go home after that because I knew that I would have to deal with Mitch, and I didn't want to upset my mom. So I figured this was the time to move out of my house and move in with my friend Dennis Burton and his family: my mom knew where I was, and I believed living with Dennis was the best way I could survive my high school years and avoid further humiliation and drunken abuse from Mitch.

My first major step toward survival came after this incident, not unlike the Shaolin monks when they started to learn kung fu. Besides the health benefits, they too needed to protect themselves from the bad guys. My life at the time was very much about survival, in the way that people who have little to nothing know every day.

I was a chameleon and could adjust my needs to fit in pretty much anywhere. When I moved in with Dennis Burton, I was used to being around an alcoholic, so I blended in just fine at Dennis's house. His mother was a drunk, and his father was also a drinker who never came home. Every once in a while I saw my mom, and one day we went to buy a pair of shoes for me, and at the store I saw Russ Alvarez, a good friend of mine from school whom I hadn't seen since the term ended. "Russ, man, how you doing?" I asked while he was selling me the shoes. "Well, I'm doing okay . . . I'm living at this place downtown," he said, and I wondered where he meant.

Russ was only sixteen, still in high school, and it turned out the place he was referring to was a dirty boardinghouse that cost fifteen dollars a day. "My stepmother threw me out," he said when I asked him why he was living in such a dump. There weren't a lot of happy families in Brockton in our class at the time, and the Alvarezes were no exception. I was bothered by the fact that Russ no longer had a real home, and he was trying to make us believe he didn't care. I knew the real truth was that he was just getting through the days—

surviving, and so living to die. In his case, there was not much else he could have done: Russ's intention in his life was to live, but because he was just getting by, he was barely surviving and missing the quality his life might otherwise have had if he had money or means. Russ was a kid who many times had to make adult decisions, and his options were few. He was still young, with little life experience, and the only option he had was simply to try the best way he knew how. It was sad.

Many of us are like Russ, putting ourselves in a race against time, rushing so fast to survive that we overload and can't keep up with ourselves. It's a matter of time before our systems break down mentally and physically. No one can tax his mind and body at such a high level, because humans need joy. Russ's system broke down many years later, in his late twenties, and by the time he was thirty, he was homeless. He had a total survival meltdown.

We as human beings need to experience joy in our lives, and we have an innate need to be happy and have companionship. Russ had many good things in his life: friends, my family, nice girlfriends, and eventually a great wife and a child. But Russ's only mode of functioning was survival, with no training for enjoying life, and therefore he later lost all of what he had worked for and ended up alone.

After my mom and I saw how Russ was living, we went to the nasty boardinghouse he was staying in and moved his few things into my mom's house. I also moved back to the house for a short time until Russ and I could afford our own little shit hole, which we did.

Every day was a struggle to survive in the only way we knew how. Unfortunately, the only full-time position for two of us during my summer break was over fifty miles away from our ugly little apartment. Since we couldn't afford a car, Russ and I hitchhiked almost a hundred miles daily to make rent by working at a shoe store, in a suit and tie.

Many times it took so long to hitchhike home that we would get only three hours' sleep, then have to get up and start hitching to work again. On Saturday nights, we'd pull a midnight shift at his father's doughnut shop back in Brockton.

Russ and I would get back to the tiny dump we called home and pass out at 6:00 a.m. in our bed without having a shower. There we'd be, two dirty, nasty-smelling, greasy kids curled up together in our twin bed, powdered sugar, flour, and sprinkles under our nails, in our eyelashes, and stuck to our backs. We were living to die, pretty much, but we had no idea.

There is one guy I know who several years ago was building golf courses with Jack Nicklaus, handling billionaires' finances. Now he's running a publicly traded company worth millions. Sounds great, right? Well, he just got diagnosed with ulcers; his physical system has begun to break down, as that is usually the first thing to go, and I know that this is just the beginning for him. It should be said that he's also a specimen of physical fitness, does not drink coffee, and does not smoke. Yet, he's already started the process of falling apart, just like Russ went homeless. This man does not allow himself any time for joy: he has a wonderful wife, home, and children, yet he works 24/7 because it's all he knows. He says he will stop when he has accumulated a certain amount of wealth, but based on his pattern, I suspect he is just setting himself up for a new level of conquest when he reaches his "quitting goal."

Not unlike my friend today, Russ and I didn't have much time for just living. It's not that we didn't want to live—we just needed to survive, and we were the only ones that we could depend on for our existence. We were tying to finish school, stay out of gangs, pay the rent, eat, acquire our own cars, continue to support our moms and sisters, *and* try to have girlfriends. My friend, the thirty-three-year-old CEO, would probably like to just live too: but he doesn't have a clue how to do it.

So you can clearly see that pain, loss, unhappiness, and all the things that keep us from enjoying life do not discriminate based on background. Unless we learn how to live to live, we too may very well suffer the same fate as Russ and so many others.

There are no easy answers to finding that balance between living to live and living to die: you have to figure it out by your own example; but using the 80/20 Technique, you can. This is where the Shaolin warrior attitude has worked well for me: I clearly define how I am living and surviving. I think about what my choices are, and what falls into the 80 percent (things I can control) category versus the 20 percent (things I can't control).

HOW ARE *YOU* SURVIVING?

When you attempt to define what happiness would mean to you, you might want to ask yourself some of these questions.

- What does it mean to you to "survive" versus to "live"? Survival is having the bare essentials: food, shelter, and health. Living is to enjoy the fruits of your labor. In your case is it having enough money to live comfortably? A roof over your head? A family? A good job? Loyal friends? A nice meal out with your husband or wife once in a while? The love of your child?

- What do these things mean to you? Which ones could you do without, and which ones are essential? Why? Would *not* having them make your life better or worse, or would it stay the same?

Make a list and look at what you have, what you need, and what you have yet to get or earn. Think about how much of it is about "surviving"—living to die—or "being alive"—living to live, appreciating each day for what it is, what it has, and what it doesn't.

FOCUS + DISCIPLINE = ACCOMPLISHMENT

The universe and the mind are one;
the mind and the universe is one.

—Lu Hsiang-Shan

There was once a master of the Black Tiger system, a rare style of Shaolin kung fu known for its fierce techniques that mimic the ripping of a tiger's claws. The master had a son named Wong Tau. One day, on his return from a hunt in the forests that surrounded their village, Wong's father brought home a half-starved baby leopard that he had found. He gave it to his son and told him he could keep the animal until it got big and dangerous.

Wong and the leopard became inseparable, and each day after he had done his work around the house and practiced his kung fu exercises, he would head off into the forest with the leopard to play. The weeks turned into months, and the two were often seen by the villagers running together, wrestling on the grass, or just lying peacefully in the sun.

One day, while out enjoying themselves in the forest, Wong and the leopard were suddenly confronted by a large tiger. The tiger had been standing quite still watching them play. Sensing the beast was about to attack, the leopard began jumping around. The tiger was at least three times the size of the leopard, but the leopard, showing no fear, placed itself between the tiger and the boy. It stood so that every muscle was rock hard, but remained motionless, waiting. Wong watched as the leopard slowly but carefully walked backward. He felt as though his leopard was waiting for something, and he was right. The leopard was waiting for the tiger to leap.

Suddenly, the tiger launched itself at the tightly balled up leopard. The leopard leaped and with perfect timing hit the surprised tiger in the stomach with the force of a cannonball. The tiger went sprawling backward, and the leopard, continuing the arc of its leap, lashed out with its razor-sharp claws, raking the exposed chest and belly of the tiger. Wong watched with wonder at the bravery and skill of his friend.

The tiger landed on the ground with a heavy thud, seriously wounded, and fled into the woods. Wong embraced his friend, the leopard, and he suddenly understood that any kind of adversity could be overcome by focusing on completely controlling one's body. From that day on, Wong studied every movement that his friend made; he examined its speed, agility, and springing capability, and the twitch of each muscle. Most important, Wong thought, was the leopard's ability to focus. Many years later, he incorporated the moves into his own kung fu system.

A good bulk of the Shaolin monks' work is spent on focus. They study it in three ways: by practicing kung fu, by meditating, and by praying to Buddha. Their understanding of "focus" is based on the idea that the mind and body can become one.

We can learn a lot from Wong's Shaolin mind-body connection story that relates to our own journey. Staring into the face of the mistakes of our lives is a lot like his leopard waiting for the giant tiger to crush him. If the leopard had not focused on hitting the tiger in a vulnerable spot, it and Wong would probably have been ripped to shreds. Whether it's a tiger, the coming mortgage payment, a bad relationship, or something else we feel is overwhelming and scary, many of us feel as if we're facing something bigger than ourselves on a daily basis. And sometimes we are. Being in a jam where you lose your job and have a family to support, for example, is no different from the situation Wong's leopard was in. You are in debt up to your ass. You have a family to support. You just found out that you are being laid off, you're getting old, and now, young, aggressive people with master's degrees dominate your industry.

This is a life-threatening scenario, and you face a larger opponent than fear. You face depression and anxiety. You can run and hide, take drugs, drink excessively, and stress out yourself and everyone around you, but choosing this path only helps you avoid a reality that is going to catch up to you sooner or later. It doesn't help you move on. Although you might be scared to death, this is the time to make the mind and body work as one. That means that the mind has *complete and calculated control* over whatever the body does.

In this situation, you can become more focused by proving to yourself that you cannot be defeated, by remembering who you are, how far you've come, what you have going for you, and by staying grounded in all the accomplishments, accolades, and great qualities you possess. If you stay focused on a goal, even something as simple as going to a gym, you'll give yourself a solid foundation on which to build.

If it's a job you've lost, instead of getting depressed and becoming self-destructive or abusive to others, look at what's real—why you lost it—and what's probably not so real if the situation was something you simply couldn't control. Sometimes, life's curveballs are the best things we could never have hoped for. Maybe it's trying to tell you something. If you keep getting fired from the same jobs, if you keep attracting the same kind of partner, if that 20 percent of life that we simply can't control is looking more like 40 or 50 percent, take a step back and focus on what's happening, why it's happening, and how you can pull yourself out of it.

This is total focus. Regardless of whether you stay in that field or go out and get educated in another, your approach will work the same way. You're at mile marker one on your Shaolin journey: you've admitted that you're stuck in a bad situation, about to get your ass kicked by life, and only *you* can get yourself out of the rough spot.

Every time I feel that I'm losing my own focus—whether in a conversation with my wife, a friend, or a business associate, or doing something that takes longer—I ask myself one question: *What am I trying to accomplish?* I then answer it to the best of my ability.

What I am doing here is "programming" what the focus is, because once you're engaged in the discussion or project, it's usually too late to have that crucial "conversation" with yourself. How many times have you gotten into a conversation with someone when you weren't focused? What about when it was about something really important, like the future of your romantic relationship, something to do with your children, or a friendship? Maybe they caught you off guard; you engaged in the discussion, and when you were finished, you wished you hadn't said what you just said. That is not stupidity; it's a lack of focus.

Focus is like a beautiful Shaolin form, which follows a pattern of dancelike movements mimicking the fighting techniques of an animal (see appendix B). Each and every movement within the form has meaning, and not even a single planting of foot or flick of a wrist is wasted. Each step has a life of its own, just like every step you take in life. It's scary to think about. How can you possibly overcome such ingrained behavior? You just have to break it down, action by action.

DISTRACTIONS ON THE ROAD

From a Western perspective, focus is like a golf game: on any given day you can go out on the course and hit that little white ball as well as Tiger Woods. The problem is that unless you're him, you won't do it consistently. You can only be a pro at anything if you are consistent, and consistency takes practice.

Focus is an essential tool for getting things done with precision, whether it is a single task or several at the same time. Without it, one can have self-discipline and a good work ethic, but get very little accomplished. Though it's challenging to try to be focused all the time, at least figuring out how to do it gives one the ability to see each and every move, each and every step of the way.

Most people conceive of "focus" as the ability to concentrate on one thing so completely that the one thing gets accomplished—whether it's receiving a good grade on an exam, successfully completing a project at work, or maybe even winning at a game of your favorite sport. And it is. What Wong saw in his leopard is the key to understanding how just

about anything can be achieved if one is focused on an outcome.

Shaolin disciples have already learned the art of focus and
staying "tuned in" through long and arduous hours of prayer.
Still, if the disciple starts the prayer thinking about how long
it will take him to finish, and what he has to do when he is finished (scrub the floors, do the masters' wash, eat some tofu,
practice eight hours of kung fu), then the disciple will miss all
that he should be learning and trying to accomplish through
the prayer itself (focusing on conquering his human imperfec-
tions). Ironic, isn't it? A guy thinking like this has the discipline to pray, but doesn't have the focus, and therefore loses
the essence of praying.

A Shaolin monk's life is a simple but arduous one. He lives
without modern conveniences and works very hard each and
every day to become a better monk through prayer and kung
fu study. So if a *monk* can get so distracted from trying to get
enlightened, you can imagine how hard it is for the rest of us.
I have seen many people from here to the White House start
off with a great idea, get involved in the project, lose focus,
and fail.

There was a boy named Jason, whom I met in 1988 when I
was doing a Hole in the Wall Gang Camp fund-raising event
in New Haven, Connecticut, where my students did "kick-
a-thons" to raise money for terminally ill children. After the
event, I was the last one to leave, and when I was driving
home, I saw this kid—he looked to be about fifteen—walking
alone. I recognized him from the fund-raiser, and asked him if
he needed a ride. "No, I'm okay, someone's gonna pick me
up," he said, staring at the ground in the pitch black of the
evening.

When I looked at him, I saw myself as a young kid: someone from the streets who was too embarrassed to admit that

no one was really coming. He was too proud: the person that he wished would have picked him up didn't show, and he wasn't about to tell me that. "You know what, Jason," I said. "Why don't you get in the car, and I can have you home really fast. You can call whoever was going to pick you up when we get there." Reluctantly, he got in the car.

The area by Yale University where he was headed was in the projects, and it was bad for a young kid to be walking alone at night. Jason lived in downtown New Haven, and was the product of a broken home where his mother's new boyfriend was a violent, tough guy. He told me he hadn't seen his dad, a drug addict, in a long while because his dad had been in and out of prison. Jason had entered a contest at the fund-raiser, the prize for which was a trip to Disneyland. I asked him if he'd ever been to Disneyland. "No," he said, picking at a loose thread on his jeans. "I never been anywhere."

Something about his spirit moved me: he was smart, and I could tell life had just handed him a rotten apple. I wondered what I could teach a kid like Jason to help him overcome his environment. All I could think of was the need for *focus*.

Jason was already studying at one of my schools on a karate scholarship, part of the fifty thousand dollars' worth of lessons I gave away each year to poor young people. Over the next few months, he and I bonded, and one day I got a phone call from Jason—one that I will never forget. He said, "Steve, can you come down and get me?" My heart leaped for this kid: I hoped nothing terrible had happened. "Well, my mother's boyfriend got drunk and was hitting my mother," he said, breathing heavily. "I tried to throw him out and he pulled a gun on me." I braced myself for the worst. "I disarmed him," Jason said, his voice tired. "There was a moment where I wanted to shoot him, and I was gonna do it because I was numb, but then I thought about you, and how I'd have to answer to you for that," he finished. I was floored: this was the sort of stuff that is supposed to make Shaolin's teachings their own reward, and on that night, they did.

Jason had a real gift—which was the ability to *focus on what he needed to accomplish to get through a situation and come out on top*, like saving his mother's life and his own without killing the crazy boyfriend. In that flash of a second, Jason knew that if he took the easy way out and shot the man, his own life of freedom would end, because he would go to prison like his dad. So, even though he was angry with the boyfriend for mistreating his mother and *wanted* to kill him, Jason knew that the guy was not worth putting a bullet into. His future came at a higher price.

In order to apply focus at such a time, as Jason did, under the strain of anger and stress, you have to train your mind to break down *each and every situation in your life at the critical decision-making time*. This means making the commitment and putting in the practice beforehand so that when the moment comes, you'll be prepared to attack offensively or move forward when faced with danger, in order to save your own life.

In the physical kung fu of Shaolin, not getting kicked in the head means hours spent each day *training to anticipate* kicks to the head. And of course it takes tremendous discipline to stick to a daily routine of kung fu, which the monks do for eight hours a day (turn to appendix A for beginning Shaolin stances).

In our everyday lives, "danger" can mean the loss of a job. What if you are the family provider, you come into work, and they tell you that they are downsizing—your position is being eliminated. Your whole life has just been turned upside down. You lose sleep, you don't know what you are going to do, and you get depressed. Or worse, you just find out one of your children has terminal cancer. Your depression might lead you to start drinking, doing drugs, or taking part in some other self-destructive behavior just to avoid it all.

My point is this: Pain is pain, pressure is pressure, and it hits us in many different forms. When it does, you have only two choices about how to handle it. One, you can fold, or, two, you can become what I call the "mental warrior," which takes intense *focus* and *discipline*. Being a mental warrior means pulling out of depression and anger by getting focused as you remember who you are and taking more practical steps toward the next leg of your life—finding a new job no matter what because your life is no longer about just you now that you have a family, or doing research and identifying the best care you can find for your sick child while he or she is alive.

I have thought many times that I could handle anything negative that might come up in my life except losing one of my sons. However, I know that if one of them died, I would still have two other children and a wife who would need my love and support, and knowing this, I would force myself to take the focus off how much pain and sadness I was feeling, and focus instead on taking care of my family. Even if I didn't have other children, I would need to direct my focus toward loving and supporting my wife through the terrible process of losing the child. If I had neither a wife nor other children, I would force myself to focus on taking up a cause, perhaps working for a charity dedicated to whatever my child had suffered from, so that I might spend a lot of my remaining life fighting to help others who had the same illness. I would get out more, get a new hobby, keep busy; this would help me to get regrounded and to remember who I was before the child died, and what I wanted to accomplish by having that child in the first place, and how that had changed, if at all. This is called taking charge, instead of letting a painful and difficult situation keep you from living your life (see chapter 10, on closure).

I know that even if someone else's life has ended, or I've lost something dear to me, *my life isn't over, and neither is the pain I will have to endure before it is,* so training for an attack or a loss will *always* serve me to be prepared for more pain. The only way to get good at handling these natural dynamics of life that sometimes curveball into our own is by practicing. Focus on some kind of bad situation happening—one that you think you'd never be able to overcome. What would you do? How could you handle the painful situation and turn it into something positive, where you're either helping yourself or helping someone else?

Shaolin warriors experience physical and mental trials all the time. Martial arts training is an extremely painful combination of mental and physical exertion, and I know in my own life that it would be much easier for me to say, "I am already a master, why do I need to keep practicing kung fu?" and not push myself to my physical limits. But I don't stop, because I know I have to stay *mentally trained in the warrior arts* in order to deal with the potential pain and attack that is always lurking around the next corner in life. When an event comes up and I feel scared and nervous, instead of getting distracted and retreating into that dark place we all know so well, I remember who I am, why I'm there, and then attack the situation like a Shaolin fighting monk.

THIRTY YEARS OF FOCUS, ONE DAY TO PROVE IT

Though I had studied martial arts for thirty years by 1996, it was an invitation to China that made clear all of my work spent on focusing in tough situations.

A medical doctor named Robert Sporn, who studied kung fu under one of my students, had spent time in China and spoken to the Chinese about his study of Shaolin in the United States. They were fascinated that someone in the West would be teaching their art to non-Chinese, as far fewer Westerners studied it in the 1990s than now. Officials connected with the Shaolin temple began to investigate how I had come not only to study with Shaolin grand masters in America, but also to earn under their tutelage, by that time, an eighth-degree black belt.

The Chinese are very methodical in their business practices, just as they are in their mastery of Shaolin. After the initial query from the agency in Shanghai that had inquired about my practice, eight months of correspondence ensued. Finally I was invited to visit the Shaolin temple, thirteen kilometers from Deng Feng, known as the birthplace of Shaolin monks, presumably so that the abbot, Shi Yong-Xin, could see me for himself. So in 1996 I set out for China to explore what I didn't already know about Shaolin. Who knew that the kid from the Richmond Street housing projects was going to go to China to see the root of the art that had changed his life? Certainly not the kid himself.

After a twenty-four-hour flight I found myself being escorted through Shanghai and Beijing, and finally to the Shaolin temple, by a Chinese guide named Jing Jing. There, Shi Yong-Xin, the best-known monk at the world's most famous martial arts temple and an extremely powerful religious leader in China, was to meet with me.

The temple—which sits at the base of Song Shan Mountain, itself part of the holiest mountain range in China—was an awesome sight. Seeing it in photographs had not prepared me for the real thing. Ancient and majestic, it had a grace surrounding its red brick walls and old stone steps that I could almost feel under my skin. I sat beside the abbot in his private chambers, a great honor. With his hands folded in front of him on the table, he sat calmly in a simple wooden chair. During our meeting, Jing Jing translated, since the abbot does not speak English, and it was clear that both Jing Jing and I were nervous. He stuttered a little, from what I could make out in Mandarin, and I found myself stammering too.

My experiences working with different grand masters have taught me that one definitely does not get a second chance to make a first impression with the Chinese. In particular, Shaolin monks are intuitive, and can see right through someone whose speech or actions are not honest. They are thoughtful, calm, and in the case of the abbot, extremely wise and somewhat ethereal. Shi Yong-Xin appeared ageless, and in fact, no one seemed to know how old he was, as though this was just one of the many secrets the temple held.

The abbot is the like the pope of China, the number one in charge of all Shaolin martial arts, and he is a symbol of China itself in a way. He asked me a lot of questions about life in the United States and how I taught and mentored children, and when he was finished, he stood up, and I understood the meeting to be over. My confidence and my ability to focus on this amazing situation suddenly began to waver. I thought, That's it? I must have done something wrong. Before the meeting, I knew that every word I spoke was going to be evaluated by the abbot, so his silence and dismissal really threw me for a loop. I expected so much more, so instead of seeing the situation for what it was—having accomplished an amazing meeting—I was already getting down about it. That was the moment to remind myself *what I was trying to accomplish*. Just being in his presence was unbelievable, and no matter what, I had conveyed how much respect I had for Shaolin, and how important it was to be able to share it with others, because doing so had changed my life. That was why I was there, and I'd done that.

As it turned out, Shi Yong-Xin thought enough of me to invite me back to the sacred training grounds of the Shaolin monks, which few people outside the temple have ever seen. He had two of his disciples perform elaborate five-animal forms for me with an execution that was so flawless I was slack jawed. I bowed, thanked him for his time and attention, and prepared to leave.

As I did, the abbot gestured for me to perform for the four of them. It was like a bad dream where you are in class with no clothes on and you think you don't know the answers to the test: I had demonstrated Shaolin forms in front of ten thousand people before, but now, I felt I knew nothing—in my mind, it was just as bad as being naked in public.

My ass was on the line, as was my credibility. I felt empty, and for a moment, the old demons of failure and pain came rushing back. Defying my brain to screw this once-in-a-lifetime chance up, I reached for my focus, and remembered what was at stake and *what I was trying to accomplish* (to show the abbot just what an American Shaolin martial artist could do, so that I might get his blessing, which would allow me to share my abilities and what I'd learned with even more people).

The "iron wire" is from the oldest traditions and seldom taught to non-Chinese artists. I had learned it from one of my masters, and it had taken several years to perfect. When I emerged from the haze of my concentration, the abbot was looking at me with an expression neither happy nor sad, neither admiring nor embarrassed; but he was really looking at me.

The next day, as I prepared to return to the United States, the minister of travel in Deng Feng came to see me, and handed me a small red booklet. It was from the abbot. Inside, my photo was displayed alongside many Chinese characters that I could not read; the director translated, and his eyes widened as he read. The Shaolin temple, and the abbot himself, now recognized me as a master of the Shaolin arts. "I cannot recall another time in the temple's fifteen-hundred-year history," the translator said, "that a non-Asian man was named master."

We stared at the booklet, then at each other, then at the booklet again. He smiled genuinely. This was like winning the gold, I thought. My ability to focus in a challenging situation had brought results I had never expected, or thought I could accomplish on my own. In answering the question *What is it that I am trying to accomplish*? I turned thirty years of intense study and practice into significant recognition that would start a whole new chapter in my life and affect the lives of many others.

I was finally learning to focus on the "entire hand" Bruce Lee talked about, not the "finger."

The experience reminded me of a story told to me by one of my masters. A young boy approached a Shaolin monk and asked if he could become a Shaolin disciple, and become the very best of disciples. He then asked how long it would take for him to become "that good." The master replied: "Ten years at least." The want-to-be monk said, "Ten years is a long time." He then asked, "How long will it take if I study twice as hard as anyone else?" The master replied, "Twenty years." The boy now asked, "What if I practice day and night?" The master replied, "Thirty years." Totally frustrated, the boy asked, "Master, why is it that each time I say I will work harder, you tell me it will take longer?" The Shaolin master smiled at the boy and said, "The answer is clear: when one eye is fixed only on the destination, there is only one eye left to find the way."

ON MEDITATION

Every martial art is attached to a complete Eastern philosophy that includes meditation as part of the practice. Many monks sit for hours each day, doing absolutely nothing besides clearing their minds and praying. The Dalai Lama says that he does four hours of meditation every morning before starting his day, which means that he gets up at 3:30 a.m. I realize that most of us in the West, with our busy lives, have little time to sit down for an hour or two to clear our minds and get centered, so I recommend a different approach to "meditation."

Instead of saying that you have "no time" to meditate—you've got kids, a job, many responsibilities—think of meditation in a different way. Meditations can be things you do all day, every day, that in a way clear your mind of stress by bringing you peace or joy, like spending a half hour at night reading to your kids, going for a run, or being alone with a good book. You will be "meditating" without even knowing it: "meditation" can be whatever works for you, as long as you remain truly focused on that task.

Recognize that you need to give yourself some head-clearing space every day, or at least a few times a week, whatever that means to you. This is vital to your mental health.

THE ART OF DISCIPLINE

*Live a well-thought-out, disciplined life
and you will live forever.*

—SHAOLIN PHILOSOPHY

I cannot tell you that having discipline will guarantee success, but I can tell you that the lack of it guarantees failure. I say this because a person can work very hard at doing something, yet still not accomplish anything. Accomplishing goals in our lives requires a combination of discipline and focus: discipline requires continual focus, and being able to focus requires continual discipline. It's like a hand and its fingers. The hand is much more functional with the fingers, and the fingers are much more useful with the hand. But technically, each can "exist" without the other. It's just that neither will work very well . . . or at all.

MONK FOR A MINUTE

I first became aware of the ideas behind "Monk for a Minute" when I studied with a very old, thoughtful, and wise monk on one of my annual visits to the Shaolin temple. One day when we were training, I asked him how he had come to be a Shaolin monk. He told me that as a little boy, he had heard all the great stories about the heroes of Shaolin, and hoped that he would someday be a great Shaolin warrior monk. However, he remembered, staring off into the distance with what could be called a beatific smile, what he expected and what he actually did when he was allowed to enter the Shaolin temple were very different from what he had conjured up in his mind as a small boy.

The old monk told me that training in the temple system

was much more difficult that he had ever imagined. He didn't like it at all, and considered quitting many times. I was very surprised that he shared this with me. Then he said that creating for himself the willpower to stay and become a monk required great change on his part, in order to continue with his training.

I asked him what had made the difference for him—what had stopped him from quitting. "In addition to attaining enlightenment," he said, "each and every day I received more and more education on why it was so important to be a Shaolin Buddhist monk, and that as a Buddhist monk I would have a greater ability to contribute to ridding the world of misery."

I was floored. Who was so unselfish?

"Master," I said, "I know that human nature is to not do the difficult tasks in life, especially when it comes to great sacrifice, so what did you do to combat your resistance to it?" He answered with a remedy that sounded peculiar to me at first, but then made perfect sense. My teacher explained that he would talk to himself; he would first ask himself, "What would my master say?" or "How would he handle this?" Hence the phrase "Monk for a Minute."

"I talk to myself," he continued. "I argue with myself: I first say to myself, 'Why do I want to do this?' Then I answer myself the way I think my master would answer it. This always gives me the right answer."

The beautiful thing about "Monk for a Minute" is its multiple uses. I put this technique into play in just about every conflict-driven situation I find myself in, be it one that requires focus, discipline, or emotional management, like anger.

If you think back to caveman times, you can understand that discipline wasn't a word; it was simply an act of doing something that required work. It was learned through practice and observation of elders in a clan, and practiced out of necessity for survival. Discipline wouldn't exist if it were not needed.

In modern times, we need to eat, we need to have clothes, we need to have transportation, and we need to have a home to live in. We also need to have joy, companionship, and happiness in our lives. These are our basic requirements in life, and everything beyond that is a luxury. Just to attain the basics, we need to make money, and it takes a *tremendous* amount of discipline just to provide these things for ourselves, never mind a family. If you want to raise the bar and go for luxuries like eating in nice restaurants, having nicer clothes to wear and a fancier car to drive when you eat in the nice restaurants, owning a bigger house, or taking more elaborate vacations, this requires a whole other ball game of discipline: one that's even more focused.

What do you want in life? That's the real question, because once you know that, you'll have a goal, and once you have a goal, you have direction. Then, if you just apply a little focus and discipline to that direction, you'll be able to achieve whatever you want, unless, of course, you're confusing activity with accomplishment.

ACTIVITY VERSUS ACCOMPLISHMENT

"Activity" describes all the running around we do in life. You know the expression "going around in circles"? This is basically the same thing. We can work very hard at something, be very focused on a specific task or goal, but get nothing "accomplished."

Maybe you take on certain tasks but you don't really want to accomplish them. Why not? Because in the end it might mean an additional commitment you don't want to make or need to have. Therefore, you put in the time, you work hard, and in the end you don't get the job done. This way you can say, "I tried to do it, but I couldn't."

If you are totally focused on accomplishing something and it does not happen, it usually means you left out a few steps, or at least one. It takes knowledge to make something happen, to accomplish an outcome, reach a goal. Say that oil prices have gone up, but I still need oil. I'm very disciplined and focused on getting some oil, but I don't want to pay the going rate, or I can't. That day, I turn on the TV and hear that "America's digging for more oil resources," so I get a shovel and start digging in my backyard. Unless I live in the Middle East, I'm not going to find any. Now, I am very disciplined in my endeavor to find oil, but this doesn't matter: I will mostly likely die trying, in my backyard.

Once, in a conversation with James Wally, a close friend and student of mine, and a well-respected businessman, I talked about what I had thought was a sure business endeavor that didn't work out as I had hoped. I explained to him how frustrated I was because the project I had worked very hard on for so long didn't come to fruition. I had been what I considered to be disciplined, working very hard to complete tasks during the project to see it to completion. I have never forgotten his response. "Steve," he said, "a lot of people work hard." Then he was quiet. What he meant was, a lot of people work hard, but not as many of them are successful. I was active, but I was not accomplishing what I needed to.

Thus, "activity" in my case meant going through the motions of doing something, as I did with my failed business effort. Accomplishment would have meant getting the job done.

I remember telling one of my Shaolin masters that I had

been working very hard on my Shaolin forms, and that I would really like to learn the "double broad swords," a more advanced level of sword fighting. Unlike the businessman, he didn't tell me that a lot of people work hard and want to learn swords when they don't deserve to; instead he responded in a Shaolin manner, by nodding and then not teaching me the double broad swords for another two years.

I already knew that the monks' way is not to tell someone what he or she is doing or saying is wrong. Instead, Shaolin is supposed to show you how to do something the right way once, when you're ready, and then let you fail at something time and again, until you realize and *accomplish* the correct way. The gaining of personal awareness is a huge part of Shaolin: you have to figure things out by yourself, or they won't make sense. It's sort of like when you begin therapy, and at first the therapist won't tell you anything about yourself, even though you suspect he or she is looking right through your soul and could easily analyze you after a session or two. Eventually you start to make observations about yourself through the therapy process, but if the therapist told you everything that he or she intuited about you at first, it wouldn't make sense to you because you wouldn't be ready to learn it.

Neither Shaolin nor traditional Western psychotherapy can make you better or more disciplined in and of themselves: just like my master not teaching me broadswords when I wasn't ready, you won't be able to create the discipline you need to get things done in your life until you know how to differentiate between your own activities and accomplishments, and then apply the discipline and focus necessary to accomplish your goals.

Think about how we function as leaders or managers. How often have you been frustrated that you have someone working for you whom you can't get to respond and do his or her job in a focused way? All the motivational books in China, all the tapes and seminars by the likes of Zig Ziglar, Dale Carnegie, and Tony Robbins, aren't going to teach a person to be disciplined without taking the steps to understand what discipline is and why it is important. He or she has to *want* to be disciplined. Some of us learn what that means early, and some of us don't, but most of us have heard that we *should* have discipline—too many times.

DISCIPLINE AT ANY AGE

I don't think there is anyone reading this that hasn't lived his or her whole life listening to older people lecture that you have to have discipline to succeed at anything. I would venture to think that if you are a teenager reading this, you are most likely sick of hearing it, and if you're an adult, you don't need to hear it again. Perhaps you think you wouldn't have gotten this far in life if you didn't have discipline.

It's interesting to me to recognize the number of parents that I have worked with who tell me that their children are undisciplined, and that they don't understand why. What's even more interesting is that many of the parents are very successful financially or otherwise, and evidently had great discipline themselves. But somehow, they were unable to pass this on to their children.

Practicing discipline is like working out, only more intense and, eventually, at least as rewarding. Overall success in life requires that you "work out" with discipline in all the important areas: financial, educational, self-worth, familial, spiritual, philanthropic, and whatever other elements are important to you. Discipline is like a muscle: the more you practice it, the bigger it gets. Exercising discipline usually involves doing the things you don't want to do. Who wants to work more, or harder, or get more educated about something he or she is already getting paid to do? Or it may mean that you must spend less, save more, and give up material or unnecessary things to buy something else (a house, a piece of property, schooling). From a spiritual perspective, exercising discipline may mean spending more time at your place of worship, reading and learning more about your religion, or practicing its doctrines more.

All things that you wish to improve upon require spending more time and energy to accomplish. This all requires great focus, effort, and sacrifice. The only way this process will seem easier is if you do the task more; this turns it from something you have to actively *try to do* into *second nature*—like brushing your teeth, eating, or sleeping—and when something is part of your usual routine, it is less painful.

There is a formula I can suggest that will help you decide which areas of your life most require your attention to discipline. It is similar to the exercise I teach students to help them identify and eliminate weaknesses in their behavior, because both situations require you to take the time to identify and examine behaviors that are holding you back.

First, look at the areas of importance in your life, like money, your family, your spirituality, the way you show love, your sense of philanthropy, and other areas of your life that are most significant to you.

Second, list them in order of importance. Which has suffered from *activity but not accomplishment* the most? I would not start with a list of more than five, and suggest beginning with the first one that comes to mind. Then file the rest away for the moment. Next, list five things *you can do to improve that first area you chose to work on*. Now this is where the focus and discipline come into play, and it will take great effort on your part to execute the five things you chose to get you to a place that will dramatically improve what it is you have chosen.

When you are starting to see good results in your first area needing discipline, go on to the second. When you go through these steps, you will see that some are easier than others. They will all be difficult, however: if these things were not hard for you to accomplish, you would have been doing them successfully already. That is why it is important to list them out the way that I have described—clearly seeing what you have ahead of you makes the areas in which you are undisciplined more difficult to overlook. It is easy to ignore what we can't see, or have decided not to see.

It is crucial that you don't choose more than one disciplinary area at a time to address. Taking on too many will result in failure, and it will give you an *excuse* for that failure. "I worked on practicing the piano/being kinder to my wife/being patient with my son/learning to manage my money all at once and it was too overwhelming." No one can work simultaneously on all of the things he or she is afraid to fail at—not even the monks. That's why the monks do everything in its time and place: they learn patience, and in their kung fu practice, they start with one form at a time, and when they are proficient at that one form, they start on another.

We as people have little patience, especially when it comes to changing our behavior. We must learn to have patience and perseverance, and this means mastering one form at a time—whether it's kung fu or day-to-day behavior.

SELF-WORTH COMES FROM
SELF-EXAMINATION

You cannot give what you don't possess yourself,
and you cannot possess
what you were not given.

—SHAOLIN SAYING

If you're old enough to read this, then your self-worth has already been defined. From very early on in our lives, self-worth is the platform for our behavior and the motivator that unconsciously dictates who and what we are going to be for the rest of our lives. It governs everything we do, from how we dress, to the personal relationships we have, to the jobs we choose and the choices we make.

It is easy to get caught up in thinking you should be smarter, prettier, better, richer, faster, younger, sexier, or more successful: but wishing for these things can give you a massive low-self-esteem headache that lasts for years.

We really have little to no say in how our self-worth will develop: we don't do the programming. Instead, parents, relatives, and teachers do it for us. For instance, think about something you did, or still do, that you hate, each and every time you do it. Then think about where the habit might have come from. Maybe you grind your teeth in public, bite your nails, bite down on your fork when you eat, trip over someone's feet every time you walk by, or become shy or quiet around strangers. Nine times out of ten, whatever the behavior is today, your parents and your older siblings negatively reinforced it. Some or all of them probably pointed out the behavior to you *over and over again*, until you were *so* self-conscious about it that through negative reinforcement you continued to do it automatically—and maybe still do—as much as you hate it.

My early programming made me overcompensate in many areas of my life for having a psychotic dad, and for being poor. I was skinny, and standing in welfare lines and living in the projects didn't help my self-esteem either. Not being able to read and write in the third grade, because I was dyslexic, added to the problem too. Elementary school sucked and junior high was the worst: I had the wrong kind of clothes, the wrong kind of haircut, and holes in my shoes, and lived in the wrong place.

To make matters worse, I was about to start yet another new junior high school because Mitch couldn't keep a job and constantly moved my sisters, brother, mother, and me around. The difference between my other schools and the new one was that I would now be placed alongside mostly middle- and upper-class kids.

To most people at this new school, I was one of "those kids" who lived in the projects. Whoever the genius was that decided to put a project in the center of an upper-middle-class neighborhood must have been the same person that designed the first John Hancock tower, where all the windows fell out. Bad idea.

Although I had many self-esteem problems, I still was determined to be "somebody" and get people to like and accept me.

It would be an uphill battle.

I had a lot of personality, and tried to use that to make up for what I lacked in nice clothes and stupid hair. I tried to be friends with everybody; still, fitting in never worked very well for me. I wanted to be liked, and would do anything for a laugh or to make a friend, or get a cheerleader to go out with me.

MAKING UP FOR WHAT YOU THINK YOU LACK, AND KNOWING WHAT YOU ACTUALLY HAVE

Our self-worth is formed early, for better or worse, and it comes from education by people who have the "right" answers—sometimes parents or other elders, sometimes teachers, sometimes role models—not the answers we want to hear that only support our arrogant behavior.

One of my masters once told me, "What we do in this life carries on to eternity," and I found the idea pretty profound. Now I know he was right: if arrogant behavior is all you leave behind, then that is the only legacy you will have, because people remember conceit or nastiness a lot more quickly than they do generosity or kindness.

We spend much of our life attempting in some way to make up for what we feel we lack—deep inside. We try to prove ourselves to others when we don't have our own sense of self-confidence and worth, and we want people to like us—our clothes, our hair, our ideas—when we're not sure about those things for ourselves, and so seek their approval. The reason this is destructive is twofold: First, when you put your trust in people who don't deserve it, they will sense your weakness and go in for the kill because that is what *they've* been trained to do in this society, and so in a way we're continuing the cycle, instead of rising above it. Second, in the mode of seeking approval, we are needy and often desperate for love and compassion, which makes us overly sensitive to *any* kind of rejection. This skews our reactions and might make us *more* depressed, or overly aggressive in areas we shouldn't be.

Look at the countless personalities who seemingly have everything—money, fame, family, and so much more. Most of them came from difficult backgrounds—broken homes, no homes at all, destructive family dynamics, the works—so when they were young kids, dreams of success were a great thing. They acted as goals, and helped steer the child toward the right track. But when these people get to be adults, that dream no longer proves to be enough. Many simply don't understand what it means in terms of real worth, value, and life. So they drink, do drugs, get depressed, become violent, act suicidal, or distract themselves in countless other ways. Why? Because much of the time they're trying to outrun the past—growing up poor, beaten, unhappy, confused, or just plain directionless as to what life is and why we're really here. Getting rich and famous might have helped them get a new Mercedes, but it didn't help them outrun themselves.

What people in this position need is an understanding of this world and why we're here, which will give them a foundation on which they can stand. But in order to get there, they'll need to believe in themselves, because only when we believe in ourselves can we truly believe in anything else.

SARA AND THE TRAINING OF A SHAOLIN DISCIPLE

I got a call one day from my friend Mike, a state psychologist who needed help with a fourteen-year-old girl who wouldn't talk to anyone. Sara was a plain, sullen, middle-class girl who was a little overweight. In terms of self-worth she was already at the bottom of the heap. She never even had an identity because her childhood was stolen by her mother, stepfather, and uncle—who sexually molested her for years.

Sara was suicidal when she came to me, and, I thought, rightfully so. In her frame of reference, what did she have to live for? She didn't know who she was or what she wanted, she had no sense of boundaries and no idea of right and wrong, no direction, no anything—she was a mess. How do you develop self-worth unless someone teaches you about it? Instead, you learn that it's okay to be molested and treated like a whore.

Where do you go from there?

Before she tried to kill herself—or, I should say, between suicide attempts—Sara would rebel by stealing and doing drugs. She ran away a lot, stole clothes and makeup—anything. When I met her, she was on probation for her petty crimes, and was told if she got into any more trouble, she would be sent to the juvenile detention center. This was, of course, exactly what she *wanted*, because it would get her away from her abusive family while getting her the attention she craved, instead of the love she didn't even know she could ask for.

I won Sara's confidence by being kind over a period of time, without having any expectations that she would respond, or even like me back. At first we talked about my life. Sara saw that I was willing to share some of my painful past and how I learned to give it definition, and listened as I explained that this process enabled me to move forward and feel better about myself. She began to trust me more, and said things like "That happened to me, too" or "I felt that way a lot." Then I knew we were on the right path.

Sara was coming into the studio on her own more, and often watched me teach classes. She helped out with chores around the studio, and though they were menial, every time she completed a task she learned to feel a sense of accomplishment. She also felt important, and for the first time sensed that there was something she could contribute to the world.

Sara needed to build herself mentally and physically, every day, and in so doing increase her self-worth, before she could help other people. So Sara's training was slightly different from what the monks would teach, but the philosophy was closer to their experience. Monks at first learn no kung fu, medicine, or cooking. They live only in the present, cleaning and doing chores, working very hard at that, getting mentally and physically strong. They are not permitted to be lazy or make excuses, as they would be able to in the outside world; they just do what they are supposed to do because that is the way the temple system runs. Then one day they realize how strong they really are and begin to see they have changed. At that time they're given more responsibility in the temple. Shaolin disciples are constantly being tested: their faith is at issue, and all of their human emotions must be let go. Shaolin masters don't give grades, so disciples do not function on a reward system like many of us: masters believe awards lead to self-indulgent behavior.

Although I didn't teach medicine and cooking, I did tell Sara all about the phases of the monks' lives at the temple, which she found intriguing. Her interest piqued, she constantly asked, "What would the monks do if this happened?" (see "Monk for a Minute" in chapter 2), and it was clear Sara was building self-worth. She became thoughtful about her place in the world and how she lived in it, and finally wanted to be happy.

Once Sara had shown that she could do tasks without complaint and finish them carefully, she had "earned the right to learn," as the monks do. So I began to teach her basic Shaolin forms; because Sarah was not very fit, she had to practice many hours a day just to get them right. Soon she lost weight, got healthier, and became more confident in the way she looked, talked, and communicated with others. Sara even expressed the desire to continue her education. Until that point, she had said she had absolutely no need for it. While Sara wasn't ready to help improve other people's lives, as the monks do, I felt that because these changes in her self-esteem were becoming more obvious, she was ready to begin to learn more advanced forms.

Sara began to assist me with teaching small children in the studio, and started to find her own power, which she didn't know she had. She realized she did have something to offer, and could be a positive influence on others.

I then introduced her to other students who'd had similar experiences, and had been abused even more severely. She gained perspective. Sara was then equipped with a vision of where she wanted to go on her road, had the physical and mental strength to take the journey, and a sense of confidence she'd never had before. She no longer ran away; she stayed in school, began to do well academically, and made friends for the first time in her life.

STOP TRYING TO FIT IN

Shaolin monks don't try to fit in anywhere. They don't have to. They have a strict set of beliefs, a foundational system from which to grow, and a desire to change the world based on changes that first start within themselves. Most of us, however, don't have any of that stuff, so we go around looking for things we like in other people, and then trying to emulate them because either that's what we want for ourselves, or because we're trying to win the approval of others.

When I was about ten years old, I joined the "midget" (small-fry) football team. The only reason I did it was because my stepfather had been captain of the Dartmouth College football team, and even though I hated him, I still tried to please him so he would like me as much as his biological son, my half brother Billy.

At first I was a terrible football player: I didn't like getting hit, and I was scared of the bigger players. Getting beat up in games felt too much like my days in Spanish Harlem. When I would come home all depressed and bruised, my mom wouldn't say anything, because she knew I hoped Mitch would finally love me.

Being smaller and terrified of the game, I had two things going for me. I could run fast, and for some reason I could catch the ball so long as I outran everybody. I successfully avoided injury most of the time, and eventually I made the junior high team. I couldn't believe it. We practiced every day for hours. I had never worked so hard in my life. A couple of weeks before a big game, the coach announced the names of those who were going to be first-string players, and who was going to be second string. When he started calling names for the first string, they said mine. It was one of the happiest days of my life. I would finally be "somebody": I would be popular, and the cheerleaders would yell out my name.

Soon after, during one of the practices, I complained about a pain in my side. It turned out to be a blood clot in my hip that required emergency surgery. My potential career as a star athlete, and my self-worth, were crushed just like that. I wouldn't be popular anymore, and no girls would ever want to go out with me again, I thought.

This was a terrible period in my life.

My self-worth was at an all-time low.

Self-worth is exactly what it says—it's the way we value ourselves. Are we worth ten bucks? Ten thousand? A million? We typically judge our worth by asking ourselves what we have to offer. Right on the face of it you know a few things. Are you kind, loving, funny, sensitive, or cruel? Do you know any tricks, can you fix things, speak a foreign language? Or maybe your gifts are hidden: you have great comic timing, a romantic soul that's yearning to bloom, or love to speak poetry at open readings.

Little by little, as we move through life, we collect things that bolster our self-confidence and hopefully make us stronger and more confident as we grow, so that we can begin to have the kind of foundation the Shaolin monks have. Unfortunately, many of us don't have innate confidence or a foundation to start, and have a hard time compiling a list because we never learned about self-worth to begin with, or much of anything else. And if you've ever been abused, beaten, or abandoned, or if you come from a dysfunctional home (whether your parents are still married or not), you probably had other things occupying your mind as a child. So as you grew older, when something went wrong and you didn't get what you wanted (like not becoming a star football player), you just got frustrated, angry, and depressed because you weren't sure why the failure was happening and you'd thrown all your eggs into that basket, so when you didn't get it, it meant you were nothing.

In reality, although I couldn't play football, I was good enough to make the team. I was a great runner. I could even catch the ball. Getting a blood clot was out of my control. It was part of the 20 percent of life we simply can't control. What I could control was what happened next. Instead of getting depressed, I should have remembered the goal—to make new friends, impress Mitch, and get a girlfriend—and then remembered my real strengths, and used them to achieve these goals in other ways.

But I wasn't yet a Shaolin grand master. I was just a child who joined a team in pursuit of a particular image and lifestyle that I believed would contribute to my personal success and give me better self-esteem. It didn't happen, I was crushed, and I had no idea how to stop being depressed.

The Age of Low Self-Esteem

The key to self-worth is remembering who you are and what you have to offer, and then applying those things to what you want to put into—or get out of—life. Whether you're sixteen or sixty-six, as you journey on this road you can often get depressed because you'll look around the world and see someone who seems to have more than you—a bigger car, a bigger dream, better haircut, a place on the team, whatever. That will make you feel bad. Why him and not me?

Good time for a reality check.

We have come into an age where self-worth, or self-esteem, has taken a turn for the worse. Our low self-esteem can be measured by how much time we spend superficially trying to make ourselves look better, younger, taller, thinner, smarter, and sexier. Basically, this pursuit takes us from Botox to Viagra, and in so doing everything is about "us." If we felt better about ourselves, and more comfortable with who we actually are inside, then perhaps we would not be so consumed with how we look on the outside, or what other people think of us.

The media machine is clearly leading the charge on how we should look and act, and we're spending billions of dollars a day on products designed to "help" us accomplish this. We have never been in a time more fixated on the external self. The power of the media used to affect mostly teens and adults, but unfortunately it is now affecting very young children, those very children who don't have all the answers, and don't know how to value their own self-worth, and who become prey to big dreams and sexy advertising. I see three-year-old girls who are dressing "sexy" to look like the sexy-looking teen singers and movie stars they see on TV and in movies, and to make matters worse, their mothers are dressing the same way.

We all learn by example.

The human race has always been more concerned with how we look and how we're perceived on the outside, rather than looking in the mirror and seeing how we feel about ourselves. And now it's out of control. A person who depends on wealth or status and the admiration of his or her staff to feel good can become a total crash-and-burn situation very quickly. Why?

Well . . . what if all that other stuff goes away? What does that person have to fall back on then? In the end, it will always come back to how she feels about herself, because that's what's going to get her out of a bad spot should one occur. For example, take any celebrity. All you see every day is what he wants you to see. You don't see the sacrifices he makes, the things he knows, the things he doesn't know, and who he really is. Maybe he's miserable. Maybe he wants his name on everything because he's desperately trying to over-compensate for his own lack of self-worth. Or maybe he is truly happy because he had a dream, a goal, and accom-plished it after much discipline and hard work. If so, why be-grudge him that? We should be thanking him for showing us that dreams are possible! The point is, even those who we think have more than us go through the same things we do, every day. We just don't see that.

As you might imagine from the one-uniform lifestyle, van-ity or status is not a particular concern for the Shaolin monks. What is it that we can learn from them, and their refusal to adapt to the rest of the world's obsession with appearance? We are not going to shave our heads, wear orange robes, and walk around in slippers. But we can start to base our self-worth more on our own personal strengths, and how to use those strengths to best help ourselves, and eventually others.

The Bully and the Master

Many years ago, it is said, an old Shaolin monk would take the same walk through the forest near his home every day. On one of his walks he ran into a young, very fit man. The young man, fleet of foot and thinking himself sharper than the old monk, decided to challenge the master to a fight; he had asked around and already knew the superior fighting skills the old man had, but sure that he could beat him because he was younger, the man geared up for an easy fight, and looked forward to the fame he knew beating the older man would bring. There was only one problem: in spite of being one of the "fighting" Shaolin monks, the old man refused to spar with the cocky young fellow, telling him, "No thank you, young brother: and may Buddha bless you." Though the elderly monk could certainly have beaten his spiritually weaker, foolhardy challenger with one hand tied behind his back, he simply would not raise his fists for sport.

For months this went on. Each morning the young warrior would wait for the old monk and challenge him again. Finally, even the Shaolin monk—he of great inner peace and tolerance—could take no more. Worn down, he accepted the younger man's offer to fight.

They bowed, and then squared off.

Just before the young warrior was to make his attack, the old Shaolin monk lay down on the ground. The young warrior, puzzled, looked down at the monk. "How can I beat you if you are already down?" the young man fumed, scratching his head and shaking his fists. Quietly, the Shaolin warrior monk looked up into the warrior's angry eyes and replied, "Exactly."

Confused and frustrated, the prideful and foolish young man stormed off into the forest. His utter lack of self and pride demonstrated, the old monk shuffled off to complete his walk, and the young warrior never bothered the Shaolin monk again.

The moral to this story is this: Self-worth doesn't come from proving things to others; it comes from proving things to ourselves.

If we have something to prove to a parent, boss, partner, or anyone—whether it be that we're the best singer, actor, martial artist, whatever—our actions are going to be tainted by the fact that we don't believe in ourselves enough to know already that we can handle the situation. If the young warrior really knew he was good enough to beat the master, he would never have tried to fight him in the first place. This wasn't some kind of fighting competition where worth would be evaluated based on performance. This was a kid jumping out of his skin to prove himself—to himself—under the guise of being better than someone else.

What we should take away from this story is that whenever faced with our own self-doubt—if we don't believe in ourselves enough to ask a girl out, or ask for a raise, or enter a real competition to prove our fighting prowess—we shouldn't get mad or frustrated, as our bully did. We should remember the facts—who are we (smart, funny, sensitive, in shape, etc.), what are we trying to accomplish (any task will do)—and then stay focused and get it done.

Bullies are really low down on the Shaolin disciple food chain. They haven't even made it into the dojo yet, and there's a reason for that: they're simply not ready. To be a bully means you lack self-worth and try to overcompensate for it by pushing your weight around, and showcase your talents and abilities so that someone will finally accept and approve of you.

GAINING PERSPECTIVE

Sure, you might be faster or smarter or prettier than the next person in the room, but when you think about our planet as a whole, what does that really matter? We all go through the same things. We all get depressed; deal with being alone, old age, getting angry; have to confront parents that weren't there for us, the pressure the world puts on us, the pressure we put on ourselves, and countless other things. We get so caught up in who has the latest fashion and how much more money that person has that we forget we are all living on the same planet Earth as it revolves around the Sun, and that we all put our pants on the same way. We forget this when we're ignoring our kids, or when we're having a fight with our loved one because he or she doesn't understand our busy work schedule, or when we just want to make a million more, and then we'll be happy. At such moments we're not dealing with "reality." But then a tidal wave comes along and wipes out thousands for no reason, and it humbles us because just like that, things can be taken away. Remember, we don't control everything in the world, only our own thoughts, actions, and goals, so we need to get those in order first before we can do anything else, and for most of us, just doing that takes time.

No matter how many goals you set for yourself, the reality is that one day we're all going to die, and we'll have to look back on our lives and say, Did I have a meaningful life or did I waste it? Shaolin monks make every day count. They are dedicated to attaining enlightenment so they can make the world a better place, because they recognize that we are all part of the same world, so unless everyone kicks in and helps out, we'll never evolve or grow or move on, because we'll be stuck here working out our issues forever.

Perspective means taking a step back and realizing that we are all just little fish in a very big pond. Sure, you need to wake up in the morning and make money to survive, you need to pay taxes and deal with acne and loss and love and everything else. But everyone is going through the same thing. When you realize that, you'll have immense perspective on your own life and the world. Everything is relative, even the way we deal with low self-worth. So you won't look at a bully and think he's just evil anymore, because you'll know he is not. Even if he knows only how to fight or kill or be nasty and ugly, you won't be fooled by the exterior. You can have sympathy for others, and compassion, because many people are just as lost and confused as you might be, and they need help, just like everyone else.

THE PROBLEM OF EGO

Our sense of self develops very early in our lives, and serves a healthy function at first. It gives us a sense of who we are at our core, which helps us in our quest for personal success—whatever that might be. The problem is, our ego can oftentimes get out of control, which is why it's good to get a check on it every once in a while.

e•go n. pl. e•gos

1. The self, especially as distinct from the world and other selves.

2. In psychoanalysis, the division of the psyche that is conscious, most immediately controls thought and behavior, and is most in touch with external reality.

3. An exaggerated sense of self-importance; conceit.

4. Appropriate pride in oneself; self-esteem.

The original Buddha, born in 563 BCE, felt that humans have no "soul," that is, no piece of identity that survives after we die and goes somewhere happy (typically called "heaven"). This is because, he believed, we and everything else on the earth are not objects (or "things") on our own, but more a big pie made up of smaller parts, and then those smaller parts are made up of even smaller parts, and so on down to infinity.

As we've discovered above, this vision is not far-fetched. We are all connected in many ways. The problem is, when your ego gets too big (in a negative way, when it dominates other people as opposed to working with them), it means you become self-involved and generally not very connected to the needs of others. We're all linked somehow. If I hurt you, it's going to come back to me, no different than if we were in the same room with a handful of people, and every move you or I made would affect someone else in the room. In this analogy of a small room, monitoring your own behavior is key because when you make a move, like insulting someone, sitting in a chair so someone else does not have a seat, eating the last plate of food, and so on, it matters.

Getting over your *self* is about being present and aware of what's going on around you, but more important, aware that it's not all about you. Just because something is important to you and makes you feel good doesn't mean it's important to others and makes them feel good. In fact, maybe it makes them feel worse. Convincing yourself otherwise that what you are doing is good for those around you when really it isn't, is a real problem. We need to get some perspective.

An easy way to distinguish between letting an inflated ego (the result of low self-esteem) govern your actions, and being a thoughtful person who cares about others, is to ask yourself each time you're doing something what its effect will be: "How will this affect the people around me? Will they derive pain or pleasure from my actions? What am I getting out of it?"

To be truly present means setting the self aside. It's literally not possible to be totally aware of a situation if you're operating from the standpoint of an overinflated ego that thinks and acts as if we're entities separate from the world around us.

PERSPECTIVE ON BIG EGO

Though it may sting, taking a path toward change and growth means coming to terms with who you are, even if it means facing the fact that you have some serious character flaws — like having no compassion for others.

Ask a really close friend — one who you know really likes you in spite of your shortcomings — "Hey, do I talk about myself too much? Am I selfish?" Be prepared for a shock, and if you decide to use this technique, don't be mad at your friend. A person who cares about you won't want to tell you anything negative, but you will have to persuade him or her to come forth with what could be all *kinds* of criticism.

Most of the things my friends told me made me furious, and I could hardly believe what I was hearing. You might feel like crawling under a rock when you hear how people in your inner circle may sometimes see you, but the embarrassment will evaporate with time. Once you start to change some of your flawed personality traits, the joy you will experience will more than make up for the pain.

THE EGO GERM

To a young boy growing up in China—whether near the Shaolin temple or far away from it—the idea of becoming a fighting monk is a dream that many would do anything to make into a reality.

Boys who undertake this rigorous course of study become men who can never marry, or have sex, or do many of the other emotional and pleasure-seeking things that adults do, but those who actively pursue the Shaolin fighting arts and the spiritual study that goes with them are undeterred.

For hundreds of years, the people of China have heard stories of the warrior monks, and hundreds of boys have approached the temple to study under grand masters in residence. Of course, some of those few who have been deemed good enough to be accepted as students at the lowest level have failed to become truly qualified, as it takes a certain kind of discipline and an ability to separate the "you" from your self.

You might think that it's easy for monks to do away with their egos, but let's look at their lives. By Buddhist edict, monks must shave their heads, own no earthly possessions, and wear a uniform of identical long robes, so that no one man stands out as aesthetically better or worse than another. These men live in a temple, and aren't exactly sleeping on Simmons Beautyrest mattresses.

Eating plain rice and being possession poor helps the monks to be humble and eliminate self. With that setup, we would all have a better shot at it, because we'd be so much more focused on the routine and basic details of our daily lives—which would not include the latest James Bond flick, the Internet, rock music, cellular phones, fast cars, fast food, and any number of other distractions. Sure, the United States may be the champion of the free world and an inspiration to many in other, more oppressed countries, but what we don't have here is a way for our citizens to find and maintain inner peace. How can we? There's just too much going on!

We are constantly surrounded by all this extraneous "stuff" and are distracted from what's really important. One of the negative results in our culture shows up in teenagers, both male and female, as they deal with image and psychologically driven sicknesses like anorexia and bulimia. These young people are focused internally on the self-driven "ideal," which is reinforced by what *other* people think of them and how they feel about themselves.

Even Shaolin monks have bad days when they want a master to recognize them for doing a form right or for doing faster chores. What happens? They get ignored by the master, which teaches them humility, because there's no reward for doing what is expected. And drawing attention to oneself is not considered a virtue. A good portion of their training throughout their lives involves beating their self down daily this way, by doing chores and tasks that make them humble. Sometimes scrubbing a floor several times can be a fantastic exercise in discipline, humility, and perfection. You could say it is also an exercise in scrubbing out the "ego germ."

YOUR FLUCTUATING SELF-WORTH

One of the problems with a false foundation of self-worth is that you can be knocked off your perch just like that. One day you're thinking, I'm on top of the world, and things are going great. Then bang, your partner leaves you. Or you lose your job. Or a family member dies. Or maybe your kid just got arrested for drug possession. These situations attack who we are at the core, because they revolve around the very decisions and actions that we've made.

But while we cannot control many outside forces (like the rain, or an earthquake), I bet that if you retrace your steps at the more important points of your life, you'll find you definitely played a role in getting to the place you are today. Somewhere, on more than one occasion, your self and the alluring choices it whispered in your ear led you to a dark place; and it's hard when you have to admit that you are responsible for a sad or maddening situation.

If your partner split—well, you could have seen that one coming from a mile away if you had only looked. You worked very hard . . . late nights, maybe weekends. During this time, your partner forgot what it was like to have a nice quiet dinner with you. Your partner also forgot what it was like to be alone with you, because your work was more important than she or he was.

If you got drop-kicked from your job, other than because of downsizing, it might have been because you got overconfident and neglected some of your steady clients, because you were too busy finding new ones, or because you just didn't handle your responsibilities.

When your kids go off the rails, it's probably, in some way, your fault. There is nothing more important to your children than you. If you decide to become too busy doing something else, instead of spending quality time with them, then they lose many of the values and boundaries, the sense of integrity, and the understanding of what it is to love. This is because these things are learned through the affection and time you put into teaching them to your children.

There are two kinds of people who rise to greatness: those who are actually focused and extremely self-disciplined, kind, generous, empathic, giving, and caring people; and those who convince many others that they are great, but do not have any of the other qualities. The ones with the first set of qualities will usually live long and fulfilling lives, ending with some dignity. The others might also live long lives, but they tend to die horrible deaths. It's almost like divine justice: history has proven this time and time again.

The Shaolin Buddhists say that bad things that happen to us are not about bad luck, but about destiny. We set and dictate much of that, based on how we live our lives. If you're living your life in a pride-driven way to make up for the fact that you really have low self-worth, there's no chance you're going to be a mindful, present person, because your needs are always going to be more important than someone else's. Until I started studying Shaolin thirty-odd years ago and started getting the lessons it held, everything was about me, and my ego.

FAILING, AGAIN

In the 1970s I was friends with a guy named Henry James Leigh, whom I knew in high school. Henry was a little crazy. He was somewhere between Steven Tyler and James Brown, which was an odd place to be in the 1970s if you were a black man, which he was. Henry could sing, dance, and play the piano, and he wore a mean velvet suit. Around the time we graduated, he was performing in local clubs in Brockton and playing soul and funk to packed houses.

Henry asked me to be the agent for his band. I always needed cash, so this sounded good to me, and it gave me a chance to work in the music business, which I had always wanted to do. I had a maroon crushed-velvet suit that I would wear to Henry's gigs, much to my mother's amusement. I thought I was the coolest thing on two feet, even though my mom told me I looked like a pimp.

My start in the music business with Henry Leigh turned into an eight-year career, and a definite self-booster, until it all came crashing down. A big booking agent for acts like Ike and Tina Turner offered me a job at his agency. I took it, and started to expand my representation, booking single, duo, and trio acts. And of course, with that expansion went my big, and then bigger, sense of my self.

Every booking agent's dream is either to discover the next Diana Ross, or to have a recording group that is already famous ask you to be their manager. I began to book many famous groups, but they were managed by someone else. I was just a glorified buyer, I thought, and I wanted more. I knew that the real respect and power in the music business came with being the manager of a national recording act. I was getting to be a big shot in my own mind, and started to take liberties that I'd soon regret. My sense of self was getting out of hand, but I had no idea.

I met four beautiful girls who sang as well as the Supremes and could act as well as any movie star. I befriended them by helping them out several times when their manager let them down, and soon they trusted me and respected my opinions about how their careers should proceed. They began to earn raves from a national Alka-Seltzer commercial they recorded; unbelievably, a bunch of girls singing about plopping and fizzing inspired a nation of music lovers.

The girls had agreed to work with me as their manager, and on the day I drove to the Holiday Inn at LaGuardia Airport, where they were staying before flying to a performance, I thought I had finally made it. Contract in hand, I strode into the lobby, full of ego, hubris, and power. This was going to be the day of my life: not only was I one of the youngest agents in the country, I was about to be the youngest national manager in the country. I'd be famous, I thought, and this made me very self-important. Thing is, I neglected to bring in colleagues of mine—the more experienced guys who had taught me *everything*—as partners, because I wanted all the glory for myself.

I saw Desiree, the group's lead singer, waiting for me, and she didn't look happy. I asked her where the other girls were, offering her the contract and a pen as we sat down. She took it and set it aside. "Steve," she began, looking at her hands. "We're breaking up. We think you're too young to handle us, and some of the other girls think they can make it as solo artists." Desiree exhaled. "So we won't be signing with you."

After all the times I had almost made it, I had no energy left to rant, and my disappointment filled me like stone, dense and cold. And just like that, I was leveled. I felt my very sense of self, and my confidence in my own abilities, start to crumble. Now there were core, foundational issues about who I was that might have helped me to remember what was important and what I was really capable of if I had developed them. But at the time I couldn't see anything but disappointment because all the money and pretty girls and attention got in the way.

When my dad abused me, he ripped away many pieces of my life, everything from memories to confidence issues, so I had problems from the start. When I failed, I looked inward to draw strength from my "self," but there was nothing there to support me, because I had no foundation, and no belief in *who* I was. I had spent my whole life looking outward, seeking security and validation from others, like my mom and my sisters, or through business propositions. I wanted Desiree and the group to like me enough to sign with me, and when they didn't, I was forced to look at myself in a way I had never done in the past—a harsh reality. I wasn't all that I thought I was because I had to admit that my ego was overinflated, and I made bad decisions because of it.

That night on the highway heading home, I felt myself

falling apart. Rain dashed against the windshield, and I cried. Rolling down the window, without any self-consciousness, I screamed out to God and asked what the hell he wanted from me. "How many times do I have to fail?" I asked the menacing, gray sky. Of course there was no answer, and I was left to ponder my demons of defeat for another seventy-five miles.

At the time, I didn't think at all about how other people in the singing-group equation felt, but focused only on my own disappointment. Letting my ego guide me, I lacked compassion for Desiree and her bandmates, who genuinely liked me but had to put business before personal feelings because they wanted a good manager, and I just wasn't it. That was the reality, but in my head, I was rejected, and that was the most important thing.

THE MONK IN THE MIRROR

Not too long ago, I reconnected with a male acquaintance when he invited me to a charity golf tournament to raise money for underprivileged kids. There I had a revelation about how I typically ignored the feelings of others (like Desiree by letting my ego run me), because the guy I know—let's call him "Larry"—was very much like me. From the outside looking in, it was easier for me to see how I had made mistakes similar to Larry's, how we all fall prey to self-important behavior, and what I could learn from him.

Larry is a man who has done well financially in his life. I was originally introduced to him at a martial arts tournament and fund-raiser, where I had assumed the "grand master" role. This meant that someone with my rank in Shaolin was often asked to come to these charity events for a couple of hours, make a grand entrance, sit somewhere prominent where everyone could see him, take a few pictures with some poor kids, then make his or her exit. I never do that. When an organization asks me to appear as grand master, I always arrive before it starts, then stay there all day, talking to people and helping with the tournament. I generally hold a meeting with all the judges, reminding them how important it is to be fair in their responsibility and to remember that when a beginner competes, it's very important to be enthusiastic. As enthusiastic, in fact, as they would be if they were judging black belts, which of course would always be more exciting to a judge. In other words, I become a part of the show and try to help others.

We are all there, I remind them, to show support for the competitors, not for ourselves. When the event ends, I often stay to help clean the place up afterward. This shows kids that cleaning up is the right thing to do in the situation because it helps everybody get home faster. This way, they see that while leaving because you "can" is possible, doing so is wrong and means you are being too focused on *yourself*, and they learn that they are actually all a part of this large organism from start to finish—and therefore, everything they do matters.

Over the years, Larry invested money in both of my Shaolin schools, and seemed to want to get closer to me than ever. As part of this quest, he would invite me to social events, especially ones he was financially involved in. He often talked about how much money he gave. In spite of feeling that something in Larry's intentions was impure, I allowed myself to trust him because I wanted to believe he was decent, and I also, as ever, wanted him to like me. Over the years, Larry and I got involved in other business ventures together, and not one of them turned out well. In fact, the relationship got so strained at one point that we were not even speaking. Later we reconciled, and we have remained friendly since, but it always bothered me that I couldn't make the relationship with Larry work. It was easy to look at all his faults and blame him instead of seeing my own role in the situation.

After musing on the situation for some time after our last business blowup, I realized that Larry wanted to be me, and somehow, in some strange way, I wanted to be him. He knew that the respect that I got went beyond the ten stripes on my black belt, and he wanted that. In turn, I wanted to have grown up like him, with a mom and dad who lived at home and could afford to send him to an Ivy League school.

Subconsciously, I wanted to be around Larry to see how I might have turned out had I had grown up with all those things, and this kind of mirroring gave me a really inflated sense of self, so I couldn't see how unimportant that was. And Larry was so unhappy because his sense of self was wrapped up in what other people thought about him, and how impressed they were by his generosity. Larry is a man who wants respect, but not the kind of respect that comes from having money. He wants people to *really* like him, as I do, but the only way he knows to do that is to buy their affections.

Instead of paying for a golf tournament or dinner—because truthfully, he loves golf, loves to eat, and loves to see the name of his company on one of the holes as he tees off—Larry needs to go to the underprivileged kids' camp and *give them some of his TIME*. He could mentor them, and teach many of the good things that have helped him achieve success in his career.

We not only have our own sense of self to deal with, but, like me and Larry, we often get wrapped up in *other people's* egos. I learned that I was fascinated with Larry because he had all the things I never did, but in the end, Larry had many problems of his own, many of which I did not have. Consciously, I wouldn't have wanted to change places with him. Even though my issues were different from his, thinking about our friendship showed me that we're all going through the same stuff on one level or another, and that in the best case, a strong sense of ego (when it's based on a solid foundation of self-worth) comes from a worldview that recognizes our purpose in the universe relative to others. That is, even if we step out with a big foot, we need to think about how that foot affects those around us, because every footprint we leave behind changes the path for everyone that follows.

Wrapped Up in Ourselves

I believe that men like Larry are often the worst offenders in matters of ego (though I too was clearly a culprit). One of the reasons for this is that such men have traditionally been in positions of power or ownership that have allowed them to feel superior. Possibly other people—men and women alike—have treated them with a sort of reverence because they have more advanced positions in the social, economic, or cultural hierarchy. But instead of making these men kinder, gentler, more respectful, and humble souls, it just makes them think they're better than everyone else.

This way of thinking is not healthy because it has nothing to do with reality. In a race, the winner is considered the best. In life, there is no such thing as someone being "better than" someone else. We're all here with the same task: to live happy, healthy lives and recognize our interconnectedness to the world and the people around us. Fancy clothes and a rocking social life might be great to have, and they can certainly give you an inflated ego when you see what other people have in comparison, but they don't guarantee happiness.

In fact, an inflated ego more often than not only destroys whatever happiness you're looking for by keeping you at arm's length from the very things you'll want when you get happy—good friends who love you, or a good family to support and share in your success.

I have worked with hundreds of families that needed help with their children, and countless families whose marriages were in jeopardy. Many times I would recommend marriage counseling, and many times it was rejected as an option. Rather than get professional help, these men and women were willing to sacrifice their families. "I don't want to tell strangers about our problems," they'd say. Or, "This is a small community, and everyone would know." The sad part about that is, everyone *already* knows. In these scenarios, self *kills*. Its power kills you as the involved individual in its grasp, and then it gets to work on killing your family.

MEDITATION: EXAMINING YOUR SENSE OF SELF

When you are doing someone a favor, doing something charitable, or find yourself in a situation that is supposed to be based purely on your sense of generosity, ask yourself these questions:

- Am I doing this task/chore/favor because I want people to think I am better than they are, or because it makes me feel good?

- Do people do what I want them to do because they really like and respect me? Or do they do it because they fear me?

- Do I want someone to like me because of what I do for them, or for who I am?

- Which way *should* I be conducting my *self*?

EVEN IN WEAKNESS, THERE IS STRENGTH

Grow, move forward, with measured pace,
checking yourself all along the way. Observe all
situations closely and carefully, seeing all facets,
all possible sources of trouble. Use firm but
proper action where necessary. Delegate
responsibility and accept help, but not SO FAR AS
TO BECOME DEPENDENT. Do not overextend
yourself. Be sure of yourself, of your ground —
then move cautiously but not surely ahead.

—THE *I CHING*

Much of Shaolin is about taking delicate steps along a
road that is, according to Buddhists, sure to be full of potholes, which the thinking person will learn to move around or
jump out of. One of those unexpected detours sure to flatten
your tires and slow down your progress is the very human
emotion of weakness.

Weakness is a lack of strength—and this lack makes it difficult to accomplish or feel pleasure in our lives. The monks
say we create our own weakness, and that prevents us from

having the joy in life we should (and are entitled to) have by making us feel afraid, hurt, disappointed, or hesitant. Sun Tzu suggests in *The Art of War* that "it is not good to fall on your own blade." In other words, allowing your own weakness to hold you back is like shooting yourself in the foot.

Weakness as I mean it here is *the lack of ability to control emotions that lead to damaging yourself and others.* For the monks, it would mean human emotions like laziness, fear, hatred, anger, self-indulgence, and worse, having all of these character flaws and not recognizing them.

In a modern sense, weakness is:

- Using power or arrogance to intimidate others so that they fear you. It's weak because true power comes from the awareness that we are all connected, not from the subjugation of those people who need us the most.

- When talking to others, always bringing the subject matter to focus on you. It's weak because other people have things to offer too, and if you kept your mouth shut long enough, you just might find out what.

- Continually cheating on your significant other. It's weak because if you have a life partner and aren't being honest with her (or him) about yourself and your needs, it means you never give her the chance to make a decision for herself about what she wants or doesn't want.

- Always letting others know how much you have or how smart you are. (Most people who do this think they have disguised it well, but they haven't.) It's weak because if you continually try to prove yourself to other people, it's simply because you don't believe it for yourself.

> Thinking that because you are a provider, you have fully done your job as a husband and/or parent. It's weak because it doesn't account for the fullness of each individual life. Does being a provider mean you don't have to be a father, or a husband, or a great individual in your own right?

> Hurting the ones around you and using stress as an excuse. It's weak because we are all essentially dealing with the same issues in this short life of ours, and wantonly taking our pain and stress out on others means we still haven't figured this out.

> Talking about others negatively and trying to recruit others to side with you. It's weak because everyone needs help and support at some time in his life, and putting a negative spin on a situation, or trying to get others to agree you're in the right when you're probably not, defeats the purpose of working as a team, and keeps things hidden that will eventually find their way out.

> Not forgiving others that have hurt you. It's weak because it means we still can't accept that the people who hurt us were, in turn, hurt by others, and unless we can stop the cycle and make amends, it will continue.

When I began studying karate, and later Shaolin kung fu, I had my own understanding of weakness. I actually thought I was very strong and powerful. I thought that being a boxer gave me a lot of control. No one would hurt me anymore, and I would be popular with the other kids in the projects. Although I was strong physically and in some ways stronger mentally, not until much later would I realize that there was a lot more to a strong body and a strong mind than I knew.

This was an important lesson for me to learn, and it's one of the hardest elements of Shaolin to teach Westerners because unlike in Eastern philosophy, in the West, material and aesthetic success equals power over other people (see chapter 9, "True Power Comes from Within"), creating a sort of status bullying—and this is ingrained in us in this country from day one.

Before I learned about true weakness, I had to spend many years learning little bits of Shaolin. In the 1970s, my friend Paul was an instructor at one of the Okinawan martial arts schools in Brockton, where I grew up. It taught a Japanese *Weiji-Wu* system of karate, and he offered to give me some lessons if I would teach him how to use his hands like a boxer. What little I knew of karate at that point, I found boring. It was much slower than boxing, and didn't have the excitement of being in a ring. The experience of seeing the look of shock on an opponent's face when you landed a right cross, and hearing the whoosh! of wind come out of him on his way down to the mat, had no equal.

I had earned a green belt from the Okinawan school within a year, and though Paul learned to work with his hands and I got up a good sweat when I did karate, I didn't love martial arts; but I found the workout to be good.

For income, I was selling shoes part-time. During a shift, I fitted my friend Dave for some loafers, and he told me he was taking lessons at a Shaolin kung fu school nearby. He talked about the different forms this type of martial art relied on:

there were lions, tigers, cranes, leopards, snakes, and dragons (see appendix B).

Holding the shoe midair, I was entranced by the idea of a martial art designed to mimic animals' characteristics. The crane was graceful, the leopard had great speed and precision, the snake was crafty and evasive, the tiger was strong. Dragons, I figured, were all-powerful and controlling. This I liked even more. "What rank are you?" I asked him, watching him demonstrate various animal poses on the store carpet. "Oh, I've only been at it about three months," Dave said, mimicking a crane. "But it's not about the rank."

I couldn't believe Dave wasn't interested in accolades like winning belts and fights, and had no idea why he didn't care. I resolved to try this Shaolin, whatever it was. I thought that with all my skills as a boxer, I could do any of it with ease. That was the attitude I walked into the school with, and it nearly got me roundhouse-kicked right out.

Many people are like I was: arrogant, and not knowing that this arrogance comes from a fragile self-image, because we were never taught to recognize our strengths and connections to others as children, and are now overcompensating for what we lack.

YIN AND YANG

In many Eastern cultures, the balance between weakness and true power that Shaolin monks learn to master—whether they're fighting, meditating, or navigating their lives in the temple system—is represented by the "yin-yang principle," a well-known Asian philosophical concept.

Yin-yang says that in weakness there is strength, and in strength there is weakness. This is true. Even the strongest person in the world sometimes has doubts, and even the weakest person has strength inside of him or her, just waiting to come out. We see a lot of this notion of balance in Shaolin and in Buddhist religions, where one element of human behavior cannot exist without another, opposing force.

Yin-yang can also be seen as basic cause and effect, like balancing on a seesaw. If you get off the seesaw too fast, without telling the other person, he or she slams down and gets hurt, and you get smashed in the jaw as the plank flies upward as a reaction to your weight being taken away. Just as in this simple example, the Shaolin believe that all changes that take place in the universe are the result of the action and reaction between yin and yang. Strength must be tempered by the reality of weakness. Weakness must be tempered by the reality of strength. Even though one balances the other, they never truly overlap, but are part of a constant interchange of energies. Like the seesaw, when yin increases, yang decreases, and vice versa. The idea is that if half the world is yin and the other half is yang, it's not going to help any of us until we can all see the benefits of both in our lives.

When I was a kid, I was all yang and no yin. It made me an asshole. This was pretty clear when I visited the *kwoon*—the Chinese word for martial arts studio—where Dave studied. Meeting with Larry Mangone, the head instructor, I said, "So why should I take lessons here instead of somewhere else?" If I could have put my feet up for effect, I would have. "You shouldn't," he said. "Get the fuck out of my office," he added, not looking up from his papers. I was instantly intrigued. I liked this guy: he had put me in my place, something most were afraid to do. Larry's lack of bullshit, although a little unconventional, was the first indication that Shaolin kung fu was not about money, getting attention, or any related kind of power.

After our first awkward meeting, things improved. Larry

agreed to teach me after I apologized for my rude behavior, and his wife, Debbie, started me on the road to learning about Shaolin and how I could apply its lessons to my life. Larry taught me the basic forms, and Debbie was an expert in Chinese culture, something I had no knowledge of. The couple together was yin-yang, and it started to rub off on me.

We Westerners, for the most part, have not well understood the principle of balance, even though many people wear the yin-yang symbol on jewelry or get it tattooed on their bodies. What the symbol really encourages us to think about is that all weakness is fueled by fear: the fear of pain, rejection, loss, failure, self-discovery, or death, and sometimes even the fear of success.

FEAR, WEAKNESS, AND CONTROL

Richie Darsina was the only Puerto Rican in my junior high school in Brockton; he wasn't a huge kid, but he was two grades ahead of me, and bigger than I was. He would wait every day on a path near school, threatening to hurt me. Fortunately, Richie was more of a talker than a doer, and he never really beat me up. He would, however, humiliate me and slap me around. "Are you ready for your daily ass whipping, Stevie?" he'd say. He was bigger, and I knew there wasn't much I could do about it.

The routine was set: I'd show up on my way to school, and Richie would say his piece, which got pretty boring. Unless I walked around the field, I would have to put up with his shit. He wasn't very bright or creative with his bullying, and it got so pathetic after a while that some days I would save him the trouble of knocking my books out of my hands, just throw them down myself and wait silently for him to do something. On the days that I'd think, You know, I just can't do this today, I'd walk all the way around the field and be late for school. For a year or two this went on, and then, mercifully, I didn't see Richie again till I was in the eleventh grade and he had dropped out.

I was boxing by then, and had gotten pretty good. And I had moved from the Richmond Street projects to the other side of Brockton, where I hung with all the brothers—particularly my friend Dennis, the toughest guy at Brockton High—so I was far from the puny kid Richie had abused. One night at a school dance I was on my way to the bathroom, and there, on the other side of the room, was Richie Darsina. I felt like I was in the Twilight Zone: in my head, it was dead silent, and I walked across the gym toward him in slow motion with the blood rising in my head. Rage and anger welled up, instead of the fear I used to have.

Richie was skinnier than I remembered him, and now I was bigger. I put my hand on his shoulder and got ready to hit him. "Richie, you remember me?" I said.

"Steve, Richmond Street projects, the daily ass whipping . . . how you doin' . . ." He trailed off. Then he was quiet.

"How am I doing?" I yelled. "Don't you remember what you did to me?" He said nothing, but he looked small and scared.

He looked so pathetic standing there, waiting for me to beat on him, that I had an epiphany. "You know what, Richie?" I said. "Forget about it." And I walked away without touching him. I didn't know at the time why I didn't kill him after all—I thought I had the right to—but I didn't. All I knew was that he looked pathetic and I didn't want to take advantage of that. I actually felt a little sad.

For years I had imagined what I would do to Richie if I had the physical ability, but when the time came, I realized that although I had the physical power, and victory and revenge were right at my fingertips, I couldn't hurt him. To look into his eyes was a powerful thing. I realized that he had never been powerful, and had been hurting me only because I was helpless. He had probably been helpless himself as a kid, and got beaten by people bigger than himself, and he was just taking it out on me.

Each of us is fighting a sort of war against weakness. Even though we may not actually be in a physical confrontation, as Sun Tzu said, every obstacle we have to climb over in our lives can be considered a battle in itself. One of the keys to overcoming weakness lies in understanding what kind of war we're fighting, and what we don't often realize is that the scariest player in the war is *you or me*.

The human experience is as much like war as like a boxing match: you get hit hard, you go down, and then you get up. You get hit several more times, you go down several more times, and then you get up again. When you get hit again, you're very tired, pissed off, hurt, and your confidence is diminishing. You're probably lying on the dirty, bloodstained dirt in the road of your mind. Before you get up, you look up. Who's standing over you, but a person (representing all the bad things in life) who looks down at you and smirks, feeling very powerful just waiting for you to get up so he can do it to you again? It starts to make you think, It's not so bad down here: maybe I will stay where I am, and it will be over soon! In the boxing ring of life, we figure, A short count to ten and it's going to be over; there won't be any more pain, and I can shower, go home, and feel like shit. But, hey, at least there won't be any more punches and knockdowns.

That might work in a ring, but you don't get a ten-second bell in life—you're always in the ring. So the punches keep coming, and your only choices are to stay down, run, or fight back. Lying down gets you nowhere, and neither in this case does running. That just takes you further away from the problem.

Fighting is the only action that will make you stronger.

In my life, it was dealing with getting out of the projects, and not winding up like everyone else around me. In the projects, you would see kids, their parents, and their grandparents before them wind up in jail, be on welfare, do drugs, get pregnant early, or just die. Making the *decision* to fight to have a better life was not my problem: in fact there wasn't one of us who didn't say he or she wasn't going to wind up like everyone else. We all had a plan. *Doing* it was another thing entirely.

It makes very little difference where you grew up; when you start that uphill battle toward any goal—a fight, always—it is virtually impossible not to get knocked down, dragged around, spit on, rolled over, and told many times that you will never make it. What really determines how things turn out for you is what your threshold for pain is. Your ability to keep coming back and keeping your fists raised against weakness as you find your own personal strengths will determine whether you win or lose.

STRONG STEPS ON THE ROAD

The first steps toward taking control of your circumstances in order to face weak behavior are the most treacherous, and require care and thought. To make this kind of change occur, we have to define the situations and patterns that make each and every one of us weak. These are dangerous moments because of how painful it can be to look at these things. Let's face it: it's hard to admit you're weak, for all the reasons like fear and rejection that you've already read about.

There is only one way to successfully address weakness, whatever kind it is, in your life. In Shaolin there is a process for everything, and this is no different. Are you: arrogant, selfish, never on time, a cheater (your wife, your husband, a test, your taxes, you pick)? Lazy, dishonest, critical, passive-aggressive, judgmental, hostile, an overeater? If you can't think of anything like this, think of things that people who are close to you have asked you to change *over and over again*. Maybe you *are* too critical of others. Maybe you *do* run up your family credit cards, putting your spouse right in debt along with you. Maybe you *do* pick fights.

These are all weak behaviors because they are clear examples of not being in control of how you act, and they are flawed because each of these traits is *self-serving* and, sadly, affects others in a negative way. But at heart, none of us wants to be an asshole (see chapter 10, "You Can't Move On If You Can't Let Go"). We're all just trying to figure things out, just like everyone else.

It took me years to learn that I wasn't really as strong as I thought I was, but actually possessed a tremendous amount of weakness based on low self-worth and a childhood where I never learned how to really live. The start of my journey to realize all this began when I first heard about the Shaolin grand masters who taught their disciples in Boston in the 1970s.

I wanted these mysterious, powerful, but slight-of-stature men to teach me kung fu, but they wouldn't. For five years I begged them, driving two and a half hours from my home to Chinatown, where I would wait outside the kwoon.

I was never sure if they even saw me, in spite of my pleas for them to teach me: for all I knew, these Chinese masters saw right through me and my power-hungry intentions.

Thirty years ago the Shaolin masters were not interested in teaching anyone outside their tradition. But that didn't stop me. It just made me more determined. When humbly attempting to ask them to teach me did not work, I'd wait for them outside of their building, hoping to get them to talk to me.

My Shaolin journey began when I met Grand Master Quong Tit Fu (my first Shaolin teacher), who put me on a whole new road. He was the only master who finally acknowledged my presence.

I don't know what was different on that day, but instead of just ignoring me as he usually did, Grand Master Quong Tit Fu, who ran a Tiger-Crane form school, stopped on his way into the kwoon and looked at me intently. "Come," he said, beckoning me to follow him up the stairs. Five years, and when one of them speaks, he says just one word. Fu never said much after that, either, by way of instruction, praise, or criticism.

Sei fu (or "teacher") Fu would teach for only fifteen minutes of the hour lessons, handing over the class to his fifteen-year-old son, Steven, who was as arrogant as I and not qualified enough to teach senior students. Still, I stayed in Grand Master Fu's kwoon for a year, and every time he would disappear behind the curtain, leaving us in Steven's care, I thought of *The Wizard of Oz*. Was it all a charade? Was Quong Tit Fu really a great master, or was there a little man behind the curtain cackling with laughter as he counted our money?

With this attitude, my learning curve was slow.

It was difficult for me to train with the Chinese: everything had its own time, and nothing was rushed. The more you wanted to learn, the less you got. I didn't yet know that my time studying—or not studying, as it seemed—with Grand Master Fu was supposed to teach me patience and true strength. I was stuck in my own refusal to see how and what I could learn from Fu's teaching methods; my weakness was arrogance, and I thought I knew everything, when I really knew nothing.

Many times in life, things that seem easy aren't, and they teach you about how deceptively simple it is to think that you are strong when you are actually weak. At no time was this lesson affirmed for me better than when I first started studying the Praying Mantis form of Shaolin fighting, which mimics the insect of the same name. My instruction came from another master, named Yon Lee.

I had observed Master Lee doing an incredible animal form, called the Swallow, at one of the Boston Chinatown street celebrations, and was entranced. This master was somehow different from the others. He had a presence that was regal like the others and strong, but less reserved. He was skilled while practicing the Praying Mantis forms for a crowd, but I still didn't entirely know the difference. I just wanted what I thought Master Lee had.

This early in my training, patience was not yet ingrained, and the next day I showed up on his doorstep to beg for lessons. As usual, my foot was in my mouth before I hit the door: trying to impress Master Lee, I dropped the names of a few masters I knew in Boston Chinatown. The first man was his teacher's bitter enemy, and his as well. He was clearly unmoved by any early warmth for me. I tried again, telling him I lived in Brockton, Massachusetts, where I trained at a kwoon.

The Chinese masters, it can be said, are not fond of seeing their art taught en masse out of their control. Master Lee's expression of disgust that day told me I had flubbed again. Finally, I decided to shut my mouth.

Whether because of my early mistakes or from an intolerance for Western impertinence, Master Lee turned out not to be so different from the other masters after all; he refused to teach me or speak to me at first, making me observe his more favored Chinese students for months at the back of the class before I could set foot on the floor.

I spent watchful hours doing no fighting forms, no stretching, and to my happy surprise, not even any cooking. In spite of his typically stubborn Shaolin ways, he taught me a lot when I was ready to learn it, and it wasn't until I started studying with Master Lee that my training took root in my very soul.

After months of observance, Lee finally took me as a student, and promptly humbled me before myself. For the hour my lesson lasted, Master Lee showed me just one exercise. It was a short set with only a few moves, and he never once would acknowledge that I might be doing it well, or even okay. I did it over and over again, perhaps twenty times, putting my feet and arms in position and holding the squat the form required, my muscles taut but mind wandering, not breaking a sweat.

It seemed easy, and by the time the lesson was over I was sure I had mastered it. I bowed and showed humility and respect before Lee as all students of martial arts must to their teachers, but in my head I was questioning whether my five hours of drive time would be better spent elsewhere or building up my martial arts business.

With these thoughts meandering through my mind, I took the steep stairs to exit Master Lee's kwoon, anxious to get back to the rest of my life. Seconds later, I nearly killed myself: when I took the first step, both legs collapsed in tandem. All those repetitions had added up: my legs were weak, and I was weak too, having neither the mental focus nor the physical strength to properly absorb even the most deceptively simple lesson. After that moment of almost falling down a very steep, long set of stairs, I realized what Lee had done to me and why he had done it the way he had. The move seemed so simple. I took it for granted, and it was beautiful: a perfect example of the yin and yang, and a very good example of how weakness works. I had a whole new respect for what I was learning and where I was, as well as for whom I was learning from.

We've talked about some of the tools necessary to stay on the path toward happiness so far: the importance of survival, having focus and discipline, working on your self-worth; however, no matter how many life tools I suggest, you have to take what's inside of you, examine it, learn how to get motivated to make positive changes, develop the tool further, and then put it to use so that it becomes second nature.

I believe that God gave us all this sort of power to be strong, physically and mentally, at crucial moments, but left it up to us to learn how to unleash and constructively use the energy we already have inside—not waiting until our brain goes into shock to find out we had it all along but didn't use it.

This is what the Shaolin warriors know: they have this inner strength because they work with what they have been given divinely, but they must still learn to develop it early on and use it wisely and at will.

BIG BUT WEAK

Only true warriors are strong enough to fight the right battles, and to look inside themselves to strengthen what is weak. They understand yin and yang, and spend time trying to figure out what will create balance and harmony in their lives. But there are many people who convince themselves that they are invincible because they inspire fear in other people. Of course, by now it's clear to you that this doesn't actually make them strong, but it's still very sad when one of those people is your friend, and he doesn't notice how weak he really is until it's too late.

I had a mob-related friend, Tony Brown, a few years out of high school in Brockton. I asked him why his name was "Brown" if he was Italian, which was proof of my naïveté. He would never say, other than that it was for "business reasons." I liked Tony, and he liked me; Tony became something of a mentor to me.

Tony would often take me into clubs, where he always knew the owner, and he was always treated with respect. Tony and I were good friends, and we hung out daily. He was like the dad I never had. Tony had three daughters: maybe I was the son *he* never had.

One night we were sitting in one of these clubs, drinking scotch and talking. Tony was very drunk, uncharacteristically so, and suddenly began to cry. "Steve, you don't know what it's like, to do the work I do." I had never known the truth about what he did for a living, even though I talked to him every day and he took me to play golf four times a week with him. He had said he was a meat importer, and I had believed him. I had been to his office and heard him talking about hundreds of pounds of beef coming in, so I had never doubted him.

That night, in his drunken state, he said, "Steve you don't have any idea what it's like to have someone look up at you with tears and total fear, saying, 'Please don't kill me.'" It wasn't until that night that I really knew what Tony did for a living. He was a hit man for big money.

I was stunned. I felt like an idiot for buying his beef cover. "They beg you, and you feel bad, and you have to pull the trigger." He told me how sometimes they'd cry about their wives and kids, and how it broke his heart. He might have been hell-bound, but Tony wasn't about to quit his job: as little as I knew about his business, I had watched enough mob movies to know you don't just "retire" from it.

Tony and I did not speak again for a very long time, and in fact sometimes I wondered if he would now have to kill me because I knew more than I should have. The next time we met, it was quite accidental. Several years later, I was buying a car at a dealership in Brockton. I caught sight of the car salesman before he saw me. Surprised, I realized it was Tony. I was shocked: I loved Tony, but while I remembered a dapper, powerful guy, he now looked old, beaten, and sad. I didn't want him to see me; I knew how painful it would be for him if he knew that I had seen him in such a place. But I didn't move quickly enough, and Tony spotted me. We talked for a while. He told me that he had lost everything, including his home, his wife, and his kids. In fact, they no longer even spoke to him.

He was not the Luca Brasi type: a stupid man who spoke in three-word sentences. Instead, Tony was smart and articulate, and could have done anything he wanted in life. But he was weak because he came from a crappy life and never learned who he was and why he was really here. And instead of working hard to understand these things, and so with no real foundation for self-worth, he used what he thought was the only thing he had—his tremendous size—as a way of gaining respect, friends, and money. And then things just snowballed from there.

How much effort did it take him to take a contract, get in a car or on a train, show up on a doorstep, and pull a trigger, then collect fifty thousand dollars? It took Tony no effort at all to use what he was born with to make big money. People like Tony think of themselves as warriors, but they are not strong, no matter what or whom they are fighting. They take the easy way out—the path of least resistance, and in doing so, they lose the opportunity to grow.

VICTIMS AREN'T BORN, THEY'RE BRED

You cannot prevent the bird of sorrow from flying over your head, but you can prevent it from nesting in your hair.

—CHINESE PROVERB

Siddhartha Gautama, a prince from India, founded Buddhism in the sixth century B.C.E. As he grew up, he wanted to know more about life outside his palace's walls. Taking a servant with him, he ventured into the city to see sights he expected would be wonderful and new. Instead, he saw mostly pain and misery because the townspeople were poor. Siddhartha returned to his palace depressed and sad; he had many questions about how and why people suffer, and who was responsible for such suffering.

Over time, he came to believe that he himself was directly responsible because his father was the king and ruled the land, but was a ruler who did not take responsibility for the widespread poverty and pain in the country. Fed up, Siddhartha decided to abandon his comfortable life—his wife and young son, as well as his wealth—to become an ascetic monk. On that day, they say, he began his search for wisdom, discipline, and eventually, enlightenment. Although seemingly counterintuitive, in leaving it all behind, Siddhartha took responsibility for his life and the life of his people, because you can only truly help and love others after you first help and love yourself.

Taking Responsibility

No matter what you believe, we are all held accountable for our actions in life, whatever they are. Many times, we don't like dealing with the results of our actions, and we start to feel like victims. Because of this, victimization rules our life more than we think, but with great effort and by taking responsibility for what we do every moment of the day, we can dramatically change our lives, resulting in less pain and anxiety. This, in turn, will ultimately benefit us *and* the people around us.

Had Siddhartha not started on his path of exploration and renunciation of wealth, there probably wouldn't be any Buddhism as we know it, or a belief system that relies so heavily on the idea of accountability. I grew up Catholic, and people were forever talking to me about fire and brimstone, and how God would punish you if you were bad. I always wondered what would happen to my dad, or any of the other screwed-up people I knew as a child. In the Buddhist religion, they have a kind of hell, just like some Western religions, and depending on the sect, hell is sometimes thought to be the "here and now"—the *dukha,* or suffering, that we experience in our everyday life. Otherwise, hell means an unpleasant rebirth as payback for the bad karma you're accumulating in this life. The point is, whether you're Catholic, a Buddhist, or a practicing Shaolin monk, if you die and you took the wrong path once or twice in life, you have to account for it somewhere.

Shaolin monks never allow themselves to feel as if they are victims of their own or any other circumstances, because each monk knows he must own up to the path he has chosen, and realize that he alone is responsible for it. He believes that if he is disrespectful in this life to his masters, or fails to pray hard enough, or does not do enough good deeds without expectation of payback, in his next life he will somehow be treated with disrespect, or will not be shown compassion by others.

In this country, and this culture, we don't recognize this kind of accountability for everything, and so spend a lot of time wondering why the reactions to our actions don't seem fair. This allows for all kinds of self-pity and misguided energy spent blaming others for our circumstances. Many of us, because of how we were raised and the expectations our parents instilled in us about how life "should" be, have not learned to accept a situation for what it is, then adapt to it—even if it sucks.

It has long been clear to me that we create the path that ultimately leads to our own victimization, because it is extremely difficult to look at what it is we do to inflict that much pain on ourselves. Making excuses or feeling bad because you didn't get up early enough for work and lost your job, or your wife left you because you had an affair you "couldn't help," or your kids are on drugs because they didn't get any attention from you while you were busy making money to support them, are things that put a big dent in our ability to be honest with ourselves by taking responsibility for the choices we make in our lives—good or bad.

Victimization is a self-destructive behavior—a bad path that causes great pain, induces tremendous anxiety, and unchecked will most certainly lead to early death. Along with victimization come anxiety and unnecessary fear, and they envelop us in a shell of our own self-pity. Unlike other, more tangible challenges in our lives, like how to get a better job, save more money, or buy a house, victimization comes out of nowhere and doesn't have a "face," so to speak. If I hit you, you feel pain, so you understand why you hurt. When people feel victimized by a situation, it is nothing like a slap in the face that tells you you're setting yourself up for pain: it's as if the universe has somehow conspired against us, and we are simply lost at sea with no way out and no real indication of what went wrong.

However, the idea that we are not in control of our own thoughts, feelings, and actions, is just crazy. We might not be able to control many things in life—like other people's responses or acts of nature—but when we start feeling like a victim, it's usually because we've done something that put into motion a series of events that we are now on the losing side of. And instead of taking responsibility for it initially, and doing the hard work of looking at what went wrong, we act like the universe owes us something, and didn't pay us somehow, so now we're going to sit right here, not move, not grow, and just sulk. If we don't decide to take responsibility for something that happens to us—even if it's something out of our control, like the loss of a limb, or rape—we end up gaining nothing, going nowhere, and never being able to help ourselves or others that might need us.

No one is a victim, and if you feel like one, or are acting like one, it's high time you figured out what you want in life, where you want to go, and get up off your ass and get there.

ULTIMATE VICTIMIZATION

I believe that 99 percent of adult victimization is self-inflicted. Children have less say about what happens to them because they can't generally make informed choices and judgment calls as we can: they simply don't have the tools yet, and lack power (see chapter 9, "True Power Comes from Within") which is generally held by adults. As adults, we make what I call "conscious mistakes," or practice passive-aggressive behavior that gets us in hot water. In other words, we create most of our own problems. But there is always an opportunity to take control of the situation, thereby taking responsibility for our actions and/or reactions to what happened.

When something like being raped or shot happens, it's traumatic. It's not a natural dynamic of life, unlike other kinds of pain that the monks accept as necessary, such as sadness from loss, or a headache or other physical ailment. Every thirty seconds or so, someone is raped in this country. But what if there was something you could do? Here's a commonsense example. Suppose you made a habit of leaving your key in the mailbox when you went for a run, allowing an offender to identify the pattern you followed and use the knowledge to break in and hurt you later. You could look back after a terrible incident that followed, like a rape, because the person who watched you broke in using your *own* key, you could say to yourself, "If I hadn't done that, the guy would not have known I left a key there and I could have avoided this."

Even in the worst-case scenario—like when there's seemingly nothing you've done to provoke this attack—there are steps you can take to get back control. You can even start now, before it's ever happened. This is what I call "going into a Shaolin mental warrior mind-set," where mental control over a physical situation is *essential* preparation for the hurt or shame that can come after an attack, even if you cannot physically prevent it from happening.

I have lectured to many rape victims, and continue to emphasize that not all self-defense comes in the form of kicks and punches. I tell them that they can use "mental self-defense." In the case of a physical attack, this means that they should remember everything the guy was wearing, all his scars, and his clothing. Then they need to hold on to all that information: it is theirs to keep and use so that they can eventually prosecute.

Ninety percent of the people who are raped or suffer through any violent crime, including robbery, don't remember what their attacker was wearing: they aren't focused because they are afraid. Being mentally focused (turn to chapter 2, "Focus + Discipline = Accomplishment") helps you gain control so that you have a chance to identify the attacker later. Most women will go and take a shower immediately afterward because they feel dirty. But that's the worst thing they can do because that bodily information is part of your arsenal. Staying totally focused on details is a way of meditating under pressure, and it is actually anything but passive.

There are different ways to meditate, but one way the Shaolin monks do it is to stare at a blank wall. Meditation during a violation means staying present by recording all the specifics of your surroundings, instead of letting your mind go blank in panic, and fighting back mentally if you cannot do so physically. It's a way to handle a traumatic situation that will put you in control and keep you from feeling helpless. Life comes with many bad things you cannot control, like death, but mental control is always yours—a total mind-over-matter setup. Someone can rape you, but he cannot destroy you by taking your mind.

In a traumatic situation, it is key that you get very focused and apply a kind of tunnel vision. In many cases, it can be the difference between victory and defeat, life and death. When I'm faced with an extremely stressful situation, I get very quiet and assess the situation. Next I decide what the best possible outcome would be if I had control—whether or not I actually do. Then I decide what my plan of action will be, and figure out an alternative plan just in case. No matter what, by making these decisions I am actively taking responsibility for the situation, and refusing to allow myself to become a victim.

I Feel Like a Victim, but Am I Being Victimized?

Victimization lives in the friends and family that we continually talk to and/or see. You know the ones—those who always find something wrong with us or let us know that we are not living our lives right. Of course, in their minds, they are trying to help us see the error of our ways, but when we feel challenged by friends or family, we often get defensive. Most of the time, we think we're "doing okay" at raising our kids or earning a living or otherwise taking care of business, and when a mother-in-law or sister or friend suggests "spending more time with your kids" or that we should "try to get a better job," it makes us feel bad. Then we start to justify: "Well, I can't get a better job because I don't have the time to look" or "You try spending more time with your kids when you work a sixty-hour week!" This leads to "I am too unqualified to get a better job" or "I am a bad parent." When we feel criticized, it's a lot harder to adapt to the ebbs and flows of life. Instead of taking responsibility for what is being said and confronting the speaker, we begin to feel we're being victimized.

Victimization can lie in the jobs we are in, or our bosses, or both. In our jobs, when we don't set goals, we get stuck in a rut—we're in limbo. We're doing enough to get a paycheck, but not enough to do a job right. It sucks to wake up every day unhappy; so many people do this, and fail to see that they're living for the one week of vacation they get every year. Most people spend more time and energy planning their one- or two-week vacation than they do planning their *life*.

And funnily enough, they feel like victims!

Here's the deal: There are no victims in this world. When problems arise—let's say at work—you have two choices. You can stay where you are, get educated, and decide to do your job to the best of your ability and learn everything you need to know; or you can quit, and find a new job or live in poverty. That sounds extreme, but it may offer some perspective. It's the goals we set for ourselves (or the lack of them) that lead us to feel victimized in our work lives. When we are not happy with our own performance, or when we feel like we're owed something we're not getting, we can often fall into a pattern of feeling like victims instead of survivors.

When I sabotaged my own success, I managed to do it big-time. It's kind of like when a man cheats on his wife. Mental health workers have documentation that shows that most men who cheat on their wives subconsciously *want* to get caught. Why? Because it forces them to make a decision they were unable to make on their own ("I shouldn't be doing this, it's wrong").

Allowing ourselves to feel victimized works the same way. We do it because we somehow *don't* want what we really think we do, so we manage to screw it up. I have had kids who'd do that time and again: each time I would help a young person so that he could go to another level in his life, he would screw it up by doing something stupid to ruin all the hard work the two of us had put into helping him become more productive.

In my case, my problems with self-sabotage followed a pattern that was always the same. I was involving the wrong people in my projects, and each time I failed, I had to look right in the mirror because I came to understand that these huge projects were things I only thought I wanted to put the time into, or I was afraid they would fail. Once it was a movie deal I was conflicted about that fell through; other times the failure was a bad investment. I involved the wrong people because I believed that someone who seemed nice and reliable would do the right thing because he or she really liked me—not because he or she was qualified. This stemmed from my own low self-esteem. I wanted everyone to like me, and I paid for it through the nose by giving responsibility to others when I should have been more judicious in choosing people who could do the job right, whether they liked me or not.

The Conscious Car-Deal Victim

You're in the market for a new car: you want the best price, and maybe you are afraid the salesman will know you don't have enough money to buy the car you want (you don't), so instead of doing research and finding the best car for what you can afford, you get prideful, and then are stuck overpaying and frustrated. I know what I'm talking about: I am a classic "victim" of bad car deals, and without fail will screw them up.

I *always* want the salesman to think I'm a nice guy because I know that everyone else who comes into his showroom grinds him every day. I also *want* to believe that if I'm nice to him, he is going to give me a good deal, yet I know each and every time that that's *not* going to happen. Sure enough, at the end of each deal, I've made a friend who has overcharged me for a car that I already knew, walking in, was probably going to cost me too much. I used to walk out kicking myself, but not anymore. Now, although I can't seem to stop the cycle, at least I'm a conscious victim. I've accepted that I'm always going to allow myself to be taken advantage of in this particular situation. This doesn't make it okay—I'm still getting screwed in the car deal—but at least I know I'm creating my own misery when I come home with another impractical, overpriced car and my wife just rolls her eyes. I've stopped making excuses for my choices.

WHAT YOU GIVE OUT, YOU GET BACK

An artist monk made the Buddhist conception of "paying for your sins" very clear to all who visit a particular Taoist temple near the Shaolin temple in China.

In the center of the temple is a tree that is said to be around fourteen hundred years old. When you walk in, you can't miss it: the temple was built around its very old trunk. The tree is thought to have so much Chi, or energy, flowing through it that monks are invited to visit this place just to absorb some of that powerful energy. Even as a person who has spent a lot of time learning about energy in the body and in the physical world around us through my martial arts study, I wasn't sold on the idea of a "magic" tree. Still, when I walked near it, I was amazed because my whole body felt like it was on fire.

After feeling the tree's power, I continued to walk around, expecting to see images that fit with my conceptions of Buddhism as a humane religion where no beings were intentionally killed for any reason.

Instead, I saw something quite different. There are nine "underworld" levels to the Taoist faith, called the Nine

Realms. In a Taoist temple, there are nine physical levels. One of these levels contained a room full of very disturbing images, showing scenes I had never before associated with eastern religions. The extremely violent and graphic images depicted harsh punishments by physical torture. I looked at these ancient pictures for a long time: women's breasts were being torn off, and men's penises were impaled, and worse.

It was hard to turn away, and it became clear to me then that in Buddhism, as in other religions, if you do bad, you pay, and you pay big. Each way of paying depends on the sin that you commit, but at least Buddhists believe in giving the faithful a chance to atone by helping others. Since they think that when you die and go to the next life, that life will be based on how you lived the previous one, you had better try to make up for what you did wrong today.

I grew up learning that hell is "forever" in the Catholic religion. Since I was raised Italian Catholic and brought up in the projects of Spanish Harlem, ending up as a Shaolin practitioner with a strong belief in the ideas of Buddhist philosophy might seem strange. Pile on some of the Baptist teachings from all the kindly black grandmothers of friends in Brockton, and you could expect I might be really screwed up.

I prefer to think that I'm really diverse. This mixture of religious and cultural influences has led me to believe there's a path for everyone, and that each person can determine how he or she will decide to be accountable for his or her actions—because in the end, all religions deal with this. Whatever your beliefs, we are all held responsible for what we do, whether it's in this life, the next one, or both. Atonement, therefore, is law. I have realized that many times I have certainly created my own "hell on earth," and that where I have ended up is where I should be, though it took me making a lot of mistakes to figure it out.

SETTING MYSELF UP TO NOSEDIVE

When I was about eighteen, I figured it was time to get out of Brockton, where I was suffering through college courses, working full-time, helping out my family, and living in an environment that didn't produce rocket scientists. I didn't know how I was going to pay for the rest of my college education. Then it hit me: join the air force! I would get to go to college for free, travel, not have to pay rent, be fed three meals a day—and I really liked the uniform, which is why I chose that branch of the military as opposed to the others.

This was the first step in a big mistake I made, and a major move toward self-inflicted victimization. It wasn't bad enough that I was doing this myself: I talked Russ Alvarez and sixty other guys from Brockton (we were later called the "Brockton Sixty") into joining up.

Don't take this wrong: the air force is a great thing for many people, but not me. I was stationed at an air base in San Antonio, Texas, where it was 104 degrees just about every day. After we were bounced out of bed at an ungodly hour, we were the funniest sight you'd ever want to see: a bunch of guys in white boxer shorts with big black combat boots, dropping like flies as we ran around in sweltering weather. And this lasted for twelve weeks.

My group failed every inspection, and in that heat we always had a bad attitude; we could do no right, and though boot camp is designed to emotionally spend recruits and turn them into soldiers, this was nuts. Military policy has always been that no soldier should stand out. On so many levels, the Brockton Sixty did, and believe me, the boys down south had no interest in hearing a bunch of northerners bitch about how hot it was and how grueling the routines were. Everyone was ready to snap, and instead of focusing on how to become good soldiers or how to survive by adapting to a lousy experience, we wasted no time in making our displeasure known to the commanding officers. The Brockton Sixty were a bunch of endless whiners, and it didn't take long for everyone else on the base to figure it out.

For one of us, a guy named Joe Delaney, the situation was too bad to go on living with. On latrine duty one sweltering day, I cursed my assignment as I entered the toilet with the toothbrush they made me use to scrub shit off the bowls. By noon, it was already approaching 102 degrees, and in triple-digit heat, a toilet doesn't smell good, no matter how often you clean it.

In one stall, crouched on the can, was Joe. He had this girlfriend, Nancy, whose letters he would eagerly await. They were engaged and he'd promised to marry her when he returned from boot camp. Usually Joe would leave the mess hall singing Curtis Mayfield songs after he heard from Nancy. Today's letter must not have been so good, though, because Joe decided he couldn't take it anymore and swiped a razor blade from the sergeant's office. Blood dripped onto the floor from his wrists; he had done a great job of hacking himself up, and if I hadn't found him just then, Delaney would probably have gotten what he thought he wanted.

Delaney felt like a victim. I knew how he felt. We were all kids who had left home to serve our country, and get money for college and a better life, as so many others did, and we didn't know if we would wind up in Vietnam, where so many were dying. Hell, we didn't even know if we would make it out of boot camp alive. To make matters worse, I had also received a similar Dear John letter, except that even worse than it coming from the girl herself, mine arrived courtesy of my best friend back home, Dennis Burton. Dennis had come to see me off when I enlisted. As he drove up, he watched the girl I loved drop me off in her car, wave good-bye, and then meet and kiss her *other* boyfriend, who was outside the airport waiting to drive away with her.

Still, Delaney and I had different ways of approaching our heartbreaking situation, in spite of the fact that we came from very similar backgrounds. We went to the same school, joined the air force together, were in the same barracks in boot camp, were getting abused by the same sergeants, and both felt we'd been dumped by the women we loved. We were kids, and didn't know anything about relationships at the time—we had probably been irresponsible in them, and somehow accountable for our actions, but we didn't feel like that then.

By definition, both Joe and I could be seen as victims of the inattentions of women we cared about so much. But we weren't. We set ourselves up for it, right from the start. Delaney had not learned the skills to cope with being dumped. He had no self-esteem. He didn't believe he was anything and put all of his self-worth into the fact that some girl loved him. So when she dumped him, of course he felt as if the entire world had ended. Similarly, although I knew my girl liked another guy, I didn't do anything about it. I kept walking around in a fantasyland as if things were fine, when I knew in my heart they weren't.

There are no victims in this world. There are only situations that happen in life—some we can control, others we can't. But no matter what situation we find ourselves in, there is always a choice: take responsibility for our actions and move forward, fighting to grow, thrive, and be happy, or lie down and let the world walk all over us.

THE FIFTEEN-MINUTE TECHNIQUE

If you repeatedly find yourself in situations where you feel like a victim, here are some statements to think about before you allow yourself to fall into one of them again. Read each statement separately, and see what your immediate response might be. Then take fifteen minutes to think through where you'll end up if you allow yourself to feel criticized or otherwise hurt by the situation. How can you create an outcome that is more positive for yourself either by not putting yourself in a particular situation, or by changing the way you respond? Any of the answers you come up with might be positive or negative.

I never have any time for myself.

You don't have any time for yourself because you don't want to. You are constantly filling up your time, and you are in control of that, no one else.

I am always assigned more work than my coworkers, and have to spend longer hours than anyone else. My boss doesn't care.

The boss always asks you to do the extra work because you are the best, or because others won't do it. Or you may be the only one who will always do it for no compensation like overtime pay, so you're being taken advantage of. And the boss knows he or she can get away with it. You need to defend yourself to the boss, and if that does not work, you must go to the person above him/her.

My family call me with their problems.

If your family constantly call you with their problems and pay no attention to what you need, it's because you allow it to happen. Don't make yourself available to them for a while. Don't answer the phone or call them; if you are talking to them and you don't want to let them know how you feel, because you don't want to hurt their feelings, or you think you'll get angry, then change the subject or excuse yourself.

Every time I make a new friend, he or she disappoints me.

If new friends are always disappointing you, it's most likely because you are expecting too much from them to begin with. Usually, we set ourselves up for failure in friendships like these before they even start, by picking people who cannot be there for us, like our own parents weren't there for us, or some other childhood dynamic that's continuing to play out in our lives because we let it.

VICTIMS AREN'T BORN, THEY'RE BRED

For most people, getting out of a victim mind-set is no easy task. In order to do so, you have to learn to spot the behavior, and then make a change. Our suffering, from a Shaolin perspective, is caused by an attachment to who we think we are, because our daily actions are programmed based on who we are and how we were raised. And this is true. If we're beaten and abused as children, we're going to feel worthless as we get older because we'll have no foundation for who we are and what life is all about. So when difficult situations come on top of all that, what can we do but think we have no control over anything, since we never had any control to start with?

Monitoring ourselves means to recognize that we do have power; we do have worth, importance, and just as much of a reason to be here on this planet as the next person. We just might not know it yet, or believe in it. That means that every time a situation comes along where we feel like a victim—someone got promoted over us, or we just got beaten on by a bully—we remember who we are and what we're trying to accomplish. Most of us didn't hear any of this Shaolin stuff when we were a kid, so we need to give ourselves a break, first and foremost. Then we need to look at the reality of the situation. Maybe the other person got promoted because this just isn't the right job for you, or you rub the boss the wrong way. Either way, take action and make a change, or make your feelings known. If a bully beats you down, you don't have to stand for that, either. Tell someone. Get help. There's no reason to internalize the pain, get angry and frustrated, and act like a victim. That's programming from the past.

My only goal as a child was to get out of the slums and away from poverty and abuse. But when I accomplished this goal, I never made a new goal. I just kept running forward to make more money, have a bigger family, a bigger house, a bigger car, and so forth. It was like I was on cruise control. But the reality of the situation was, things had changed—as they always do. I now had a wife, kids, a big home, and new responsibilities. I wasn't poor or being abused anymore. My thinking needed to change too, and for a long time it didn't, so when I was working on some new project and one of my kids was crying because I didn't give him any time, I got mad at him because, hey—didn't he know how hard I worked for all this? Then I'd feel bad, as if I'd done something wrong, or get angry because I couldn't figure it all out, and then just avoid everything because that was easier than dealing with it. But when you don't deal with something it always finds a way of coming back to you, and being even bigger and worse than before. By the second or third time around, I was really just a self-inflicted victim, instead of recognizing that it was my attitude that needed to change, not the situation.

In order to stop feeling like a victim, you need a clear definition of what you want—right now—in your life. If you don't know who you are (that you like movies, that you hate big crowds, that you are sensitive, or hate wearing suits to work), you'll never be able to figure out what you want, and so you will repeatedly end up on the short end of the evolutionary stick. It's like getting on a ship and heading out onto the ocean with no compass. You're just putting up your little sail and saying, "I want to go over there," then trying to go from point A to B. *Good luck*. Without a clear definition of direction and how to get to B, you're headed for failure.

What if there's a woman who was emotionally abused by her dad, never had a good relationship with him, and was always seeking his approval and attention—and never getting it? Logically, you would think she would want to find a mate who loved her to death and paid her a tremendous amount of attention. Statistically, however, that does not happen; many women in situations like the example above seek someone like their dad because they base their self-worth on the ability to make themselves lovable because of the very abuse they had to endure.

None of these things—like seeking love or wanting attention—are inherently bad, unless of course they bring you pain. Were the woman I mentioned above able to take the tough fifteen-minute break I suggest before entering into a new romantic relationship, she might be able to recognize that she may be prolonging her suffering—again, as she has in each romantic entanglement before—if she is waiting for a man to validate her and her attractiveness to him.

Victimization is not gender specific: men suffer from it as often as women. Take a man who has a constant need to cheat on his wife or girlfriend. When he is unfaithful, the infidelity can be about a number of things, but often it is the "need" for nurturing and attention from other women because he did not get that earlier in life from an important female figure.

This guy feels as if he's a victim—amazingly enough—because he's built up a series of rationalizations that *allow* this way of thinking. Long before he first began having affairs, he justified them by thinking that he would never get his needs fulfilled by his wife, making it next to impossible for him to have a loving, trusting relationship with her, no matter who she is and how hard she tries. This is because he will not allow the wife to give him what he needs, and nothing she does will ever be enough because he's chosen the wrong woman from the start.

How can this man get out of his predicament? First, he must realize that he's set himself up for failure by seeking a relationship with a woman that he could not emotionally commit to, therefore taking the first step in justifying his actions, and then carrying them out, time after time. To correct the behavior, he has to stop thinking of himself as a victim, but he won't want to do this right away. He might make excuses—"I'm gonna get a divorce, since we're not having sex" or "She works all the time and has no time for me"—and thus set himself up to fail.

MAKING MISTAKES UNTIL YOU GET IT RIGHT

Shaolin training is all about doing something until you get it right: You're going to carry a stick across your back with two buckets of water on either end, go down the mountain, bring the whole thing back up to the top again, and worse, you're going do it till you fall down or make it to the top without spilling any. The presiding monk will see to it that you carry those heavy buckets until you can haul them up the mountain without spilling anything: if and when you do that, he'll tell you to add another two buckets onto the stick. Though it is frustrating to the novice monks, it teaches them perseverance, focus (that is, "Don't spill the stupid things, or you'll be going back up again"), and discipline.

Whether it's even possible to get up the hill without spilling any water becomes insignificant; what's significant is how strong your mind becomes during the task. Taking control of the journey up and down, much as you can in your own life, means saying, "I am going to get to the top of my mountain, and whether I have half a bucket or a full one, I'm gonna have to do it *again*."

You can get depressed about life, sit down, cry, and refuse to move forward, or you can go and get some more damn buckets and move on. For most of my life, every time I spilled my "water," I tried to "fix" the situation, rather than accepting that sometimes things just happen and they don't always suit your sense of how a situation should work out. But you can't control everything. You need to be able to see the bigger picture of what you want out of life; recognize that we can't control everything (a heavy wind, let's say, that throws your bucket to the ground); and then stay focused when the unexpected comes our way, and continue on.

Changing the Pattern

Shaolin monks know that if you start with garbage (abuse, no direction, parents who ignored you, parents who were great but never taught you anything), nothing can come out of your experience except more garbage unless you make changes: you beget what you bring. That's why when monks decide to become monks, they start from scratch. They need to clean out their bucket of life before it can be filled again with a new blueprint. They strengthen their bodies and minds. They get a whole new structure to the universe and our place in it, which gives them a solid foundation upon which to continue their focus and discipline. They are never victims: they take responsibility for their actions, and give themselves a break when things don't go their way, because they know that we can't control everything.

The bottom line is, shit happens, but you don't have to stay in it. You can be and do anything you want. There are many people, however, who choose to stay in their shit because they don't seek answers on how to get out, or they feel they're owed something from life for all the torment they've had to endure, so they wait around for someone to come and fix everything for them. This isn't going to happen. This is the mind of a victim. No one is going to fix your problems except you.

If Shaolin practitioners got up each day and thought, I have to work out for the next six hours before I eat lunch: my life sucks and it's boring! or My master hates me, and he treats the other disciples better: it's not fair! or I'm powerless in this situation; I can't change a thing, they too would be on Prozac. What makes them different is that when these thoughts arise, they have a foundation on which to make sense out of them. To the monks, "six hours" is nothing in the grand scheme of getting to enlightenment. They have a bigger picture, and a focused goal, so that over time these thoughts start to make less and less sense in the context of what they want. As they get to more advanced levels, they don't even think anymore—they simply move. "First get out of bed, then use the bathroom, then brush your teeth and get to the train-ing grounds. Now move this way. Then move that way." This is just like how a kung fu artist often moves around a punch, rather than fighting and getting beaten down, and keeps on walking toward his goal using the path of least resistance. Over many years of study, then, I have come to understand that overcoming victimization is as much about taking re-sponsibility for your role in things as it is about moving around the punches you don't control.

A perfect example of this Shaolin mind-set is my friend Charley Mattera, who is also a Shaolin grand master. I have known this man for over thirty years, and I always marvel at the fact that no matter what happens to him, it seems that he never lets the situation get him down.

I have seen him go through losing everything he had ever worked for, a divorce, death threats, and an IRS audit that would have choked Donald Trump. One day he called from his car and said, "Steve, you won't believe this. I got a letter from the IRS that says I owe them a cargo-load of money." I said, "Charley, what are you going to do?" "What can I do but see it though?" he responded. The most amazing thing to me was that I couldn't detect any sense of stress or pain in his voice.

In spite of my Shaolin training, I can't honestly say I would have handled this as well as he did. In my astonishment about his casual attitude—which should not be confused with having a big ego and thinking it would all work out because he was invincible—I said, "Charley, how the hell can you be so calm about this?"

With a whole new tone in his voice he said to me very sternly, as a master might, "Steve, I refuse to let this or anything else affect the quality of my life."

What Charley was saying was that there was *nothing he could do* to change the letter he had received, and that he was going to be accountable for taking care of the problem, and would not give in to acting like a frightened, angry, freaked-out victim who either can't accept the problem, tries to avoid it, or blames everyone for his misery except himself.

ANGER IS WASTED ENERGY

When you see a good person,
think about evaluating that person.
When you see a bad person,
think about evaluating yourself.

—CONFUCIUS

One day, a scorpion arrived at the bank of a river. He wanted to cross it, but there was no way for him to do so without drowning. He asked a nearby frog if he would take him across the river on his back. The frog said no because he thought that the scorpion would sting him to death. The scorpion assured the frog that he would not sting him, because if he did the frog would die and the scorpion would drown. The frog could see the logic in this and so agreed to carry the scorpion across the river. About halfway across, the scorpion stung the frog, which immediately died, drowning the scorpion in the process.

Many Shaolin masters have told this classic story to their disciples, who respond with some confusion. They don't know why the tale ends the way it does, because the frog seems too stupid for words for not thinking the scorpion would drown them both eventually. The masters reply that the stinging and killing are what scorpions do—that it's their nature. The scorpion was not to blame for its actions, because it had *no* choice. The story of the scorpion and the frog is meant to illustrate the differences between humans and animals. What animals do is unchangeable because it is their nature, but what we do as human beings is by *choice*.

When I began my kung fu training, I heard the story of the scorpion and the frog from a master, and I didn't understand why he was sharing it when I was in the middle of a session with him. He told me the story after he saw that I was very upset, although I tried to hide my feelings about the fact that I was having a very difficult time with a new Shaolin kung fu form. I apologized to the master because I knew he could see that I was frustrated with myself. He just shook his head silently and stared at me until I calmed down completely. Then we moved on, but I couldn't stop thinking about the stupid frog and scorpion crossing the river.

THE CHOICE OF ANGER

I broke the story down in my head a hundred times, trying to understand the lesson. I finally got that my master was saying my anger was my *choice* about how to behave, and it wasn't a good one. A scorpion stings because that is what it does, but we are not angry by nature. Maybe we're angry from things that have happened in the past, and maybe this becomes programmed in us, but most of us get angry for very specific reasons. After that, I started to examine my anger and rage from a whole new perspective, and knew that I could no longer use the excuse that these behaviors were okay because of the lame definition I had assigned to them: that I was frustrated. Why was I so frustrated?

It was then that I started to associate anger, hatred, and rage with weakness. I learned that anger, over time, has the ability to destroy us because it clouds our judgment, ties us to the past, and has no positive outcome—ever.

This gave me the most powerful tool I could have found to help angry and violent teens later in my life, and it was all about finding what I call the "correct definition," or a more accurate description, of my behavior.

According to mental health professionals, anger begins in what is called the "unconscious-unconscious" state. This is as simple as a baby crying for milk. Depending on the response, anger may form. If the child receives gratification—milk—quickly, then all is fine. If not, the child continues to cry, and doesn't know why no one is feeding her. The brain says "hungry," but the conscious mind doesn't have a definition yet of what "hunger" means or the language to communicate this. So emotions like fear and anger are developed through the lack, or fulfillment, of basic needs.

Even as adults, most immediate angry or hateful responses to situations are knee-jerk reactions, and when we're in that moment, we are no different than a two-year-old who hasn't learned how to express what she needs.

I remember what would happen when I was in my teens and I would get very angry. What provoked it didn't matter. It could be Mitch, my stepdad, yelling at my sisters in a drunken fit. It could be a kid at school teasing me because my clothes were ragged. It didn't matter. I was already so full of rage that I'd destroy objects I was surrounded by. The walls took a beating from me, or I'd rip something apart, or kick the furniture. The worst part of it was that I wouldn't stop until I had seriously damaged whatever I was attacking.

Most times I would hurt myself in the process, but for a while this behavior worked for me. People who enraged me feared me, and I didn't actually have to hit them. I liked that. When I was in one of my fits, ripping the furniture apart, punching the walls, and bruising my fingers, I felt in control, believe it or not. It took years to see the irony and absurdity of that: I felt strong but wasn't strong at all. I was out of control, with no way to understand my anger and no positive outlet to funnel it into when it came up.

When we're teenagers, puberty and the social awkwardness that comes with it can cause enough pain and anger, but when you throw racism and other social problems into the mix, anger can quickly turn to rage.

It was 1970, the civil rights movement had been going on for some time, and on a local level, the whites and blacks at my high school didn't like each other much out of learned bigotry. For weeks, white girls were getting the shit kicked out of them for "stealing" the black guys from their "rightful" girlfriends of color; black girls were grabbing them and beating them silly in the locker rooms and stabbing them, and the administration was loath to do anything about it. Years of frustration, of feeling disrespected, invisible, feeling like victims in the face of presumed white privilege, false as that was (we were all poor, working-class kids) spilled over big-time. It was really bad.

The administration grew anxious; they were closing the school every other day because kids, and later teachers, were getting beaten up. Soon more students got into it, and like so many social problems that come from discrimination and economic frailty, discord in the school became an epidemic.

Then, it happened. One morning when I showed up for school, the word was out that there was going to be a riot. The funny thing about mass uprisings (and Brockton High, with its some 7,500 students, was certainly massive) is that a rumor can spread like wildfire, but after a certain point it's difficult to tell where it originated or what to expect in reality. Standing on top of one of the four buildings that made up Brockton High School, I surveyed the gray landscape, peering down into the courtyard. It was huge: so big that almost 4,000 kids could jam into it at once.

My friend Joyce, a black girl who was from the South, appeared in the center of the growing crowd, which teemed with anger and hatred. Joyce, who was tall and very pretty, had been a naive, well-mannered young lady when she arrived in Brockton a few years before. Surprisingly, she had no prejudice and was nice to everybody, regardless of color.

A country girl to the core, she found the roughness of Brockton High hard to bear, which was probably why I liked her so much. Joyce would tell stories of the Klan and how they burned her family's house, but still, somehow, she wasn't a hateful person. Coming to the North, she was exposed to a different level of racism: the racism that urban poverty created, and a faulty welfare system doesn't solve.

Although Joyce had the foundation and all the makings of following a healthy path, she was young, and the influence of all the other negative kids eventually overtook her (which is a good lesson in itself that who we associate with, we are, and we are influenced by). So she became like everyone else in Brockton that I knew, black or white—poor and angry. Brockton had turned Joyce mean: on the day of the riot, she grabbed Kevin Giardino, a white kid, and punched him right in the face. It could have been anyone: that riot was going to take place with or without Joyce's first punch. And that was it: chaos broke out in the schoolyard. Joyce lost her temper and started a race riot.

The lesson here is that as good as any of us can be in the

beginning, we can all fall prey to our overwhelming negative environment and anger. Joyce was a good kid, and she had little or no anger when she arrived in Brockton from the South. She was introduced to anger and hate by her peers in the North, and she was taught to thrive on it to fit in. For the first time in her life, avoiding anger and conflict would have required that she have a strong mind equipped to deal with these feelings and the resulting behaviors. She did not because she was never given the tools to fight against her own weaknesses. Joyce went into battle without knowing the true enemy: herself.

There are many children like Joyce whom I have worked with who are very angry and don't know why and what to do about it. Many adults feel the same way. Much, if not most, of our anger or depression starts at a very young age for many people. In my case, it came with my dad's abuse and having to live in poverty. Similar situations created a sense of anger about life for many of the children I have worked with. Still others, who had plenty of food and nice clothes and a comfortable home, suffered from the same angry and sometimes violent behavior.

In the beginning of my work in different communities, it was difficult for me to help anyone who didn't come from where I did. I didn't know how kids with so much could take it for granted, but I learned that they were in just as much pain as some of the poor kids whose parents were drug addicts or alcoholics. They were angry or full of their own reasons for feeling hatred, rage, and anger.

ANGER IS A WARNING SIGN

What about people who get angry or hate us, seemingly for no "good" reason? Well, the answer is there is always a rea-

son, even if you don't know what it is, and from a psycholog-
ical standpoint, it's always a valid one, even though it doesn't
justify the bad behavior. Often we hate people because they
are mirrors of others who have hurt us, and in them we see
our past. Other times they are mirrors for ourselves: we see
something in them that we hate within ourselves.

They remind us of things we don't want to see or don't
want to happen again. I knew that my dad had a mental illness, and I was concerned that genetically I might turn out
like him, but I was determined that I would not because I
thought he was weak, and I hated that. I pitied him deeply;
still, I was terrified that I couldn't change my destiny. It was
that fear of inevitability that drove some of my hatred for my
dad, as much as it was fury over how he had treated my family and me.

Understanding a loved one's bad behavior never makes it
okay to continue to live with, particularly if the behavior is
abusive and you feel that you hate him or her. Many people
allow themselves to continue being abused by those they care
about, and this is particularly true of women suffering from
emotional, sexual, or physical abuse. Many wonder why they
are unable to change the type of men that they date, even
though each relationship they have is painful and unfulfilling.

Let's look at it another way: If your crazy uncle touches
you inappropriately, it shouldn't be allowed to continue under any circumstances—even if you feel bad for him. His behavior is an abuse, literally, of the boundary between a parent
or elder relative and a child that is necessary for a child to
have a "normal," or emotionally healthy upbringing. This
boundary means that the elder's responsibility to protect,
guide, and love the child has been corrupted by something
sexual, which should only occur between consenting adults.

When something like child sexual abuse happens to you,

you might be deluded into thinking that you need to help your uncle, because you feel sorry for him. Or, as a young child, you might be afraid and confused when this happens: when one is being abused by a family member or someone else, more often than not we know it's wrong, but we allow it to occur because we're supposed to trust that person. It's not his fault that he's doing what he's doing to you, you might reason, and attempting to understand where your uncle came from and what his particular baggage is, you might be right. But it's still not okay.

Abusive behavior is always wrong, no matter the cause. If you can see the burdens of the troubled person for what they are, or the situation for what it is, and from a different behavioral standpoint move forward, the trauma that happened to you can be lessened. Clearly understanding right and wrong, and being aware that we can choose how we react to situations in life, is a good way to begin. We may not be able to change our fathers, uncles, or other abusers, but we can change ourselves. Instead of getting angry—which never gets us anywhere—funnel that energy into something positive, like getting out or getting help. Only *you* can control what you do and how you choose to respond to a situation of conflict.

ANGER'S BEST FRIEND, CONFLICT

I cannot talk about anger without talking about conflict. One seems to fuel the other. Most people who have an anger problem also have an inherent problem with conflict, and it has usually got to do with something in the past that has caused them mental (as opposed to physical) pain. Someone you are in contact with today, or even your children, might do something that triggers your brain to respond with anger. The only way to get at the root of what's bothering you is to examine the person's behavior that upset you, then think about whether you act that way, or someone close to you did so in the past.

Once you have a handle on the basis for your anger, you can move forward toward more effectively learning to control your anger, and this is precisely why "Monk for a Minute" (see chapter 2, "Focus + Discipline = Accomplishment") works so well in so many situations. It's crucial to discover and come to terms with past injuries so the memories don't evoke fear and anger in new situations, especially with people we care about who really had nothing to do with those past hurts.

There are primarily two types of conflict, "organizational" and "interpersonal." Organizational conflict usually occurs in business or work-related matters. Interpersonal conflict is the most common of the two: it is a manifestation of how our personal value system resonates in the world around us—that is, how we interact with other people, including our parents, relatives, teachers, close friends, and lovers. Interpersonal conflict usually occurs when your personal beliefs differ from someone else's. The big ones are religion, family, marriage, children, money, and sex, though not necessarily in that order.

You define yourself on these subjects, and when someone interferes or violates your boundaries in these areas, conflict is created. That can, and often does, lead to anger, and can result in a verbal attack or worse. Rage is pretty high on the angry chart because it has deep roots. Rage is a form of hate: you might not hate the person you go into a rage against (although the person on the other end of your anger might think so), but you usually hate what he or she did. Rage represents true inner conflict: it comes from hurtful things that happened to you while you were growing up, which you had little or no control over, seeping over into current life situations.

Anger and rage are two of the most difficult emotions to battle because myriad things can trigger them. Some people knock over a glass of water and go into a rage because the entire day has been going poorly and that's the last straw. Or they rise up when one of their kids isn't listening to them, and find themselves yelling and overreacting without thinking.

The power that you feel, and the temporary satisfaction that you get at the time of anger and rage, are difficult to fight because they seem okay to you at that moment. There are two ways a person can feel *after* he acts out of anger and or rage. In one scenario, he likes the behavior because it allows him to feel in control; he has no remorse and feels that he has accomplished something. He reasons: The person on the other end deserved it. "My kid won't behave like that again" or "My spouse won't ever do that to me again" or "My fellow worker will respect me now," he might rationalize. But does this ever happen? Of course not! Kids only act worse, partners internalize the pain of being yelled at, and coworkers will hate you and try to look for another job, or talk badly behind your back. In the other scenario, the person feels remorse, perhaps asking him- or herself, "Why did I act that way?"

In my experience, no type of anger is ever good. Anger is negativity in its purest form, and only brings misery and pain to you and others. I do, however, believe that certain types of *conflict* can bring about positive change.

Say your wife is always upset with you because she feels you are not interested in her day-to-day problems, and the two of you are in constant conflict over this. If you both talk about it, and you in turn make some changes in your attitude in dealing with the things that upset her, however insignificant they may seem to you, she'll soon be more willing to work out the relationship because she sees that you are making a strong effort.

On the other hand, you might get upset because you work all day, come home, and can't listen to your wife complain about her day and what she had to go through at her own job or with the kids. You feel that you shouldn't have to deal with this; it's not part of your "job." You don't complain to her about your job—you just do it—or maybe you do complain, and you think that it is part of your wife's obligation to listen to *you*. It isn't, of course. The question is how do we learn the process of compromise?

I think you get the idea: conflict can bring about positive change if the people involved want to manage it. This theory also applies to organizational conflict in the workplace. Conflict there can bring about change that betters the organization and your position, if workers who disagree find a way to compromise.

One anger-management technique I use on myself, and teach, is to be aware of when one is in a very emotional state of mind. In a very emotional state, we can do some of our best work; we can also do some of the worst damage. That is, emotion, as a human quality, is good if it can be controlled. When we are overemotional, we often make poor decisions. You might break up with someone you love because you are momentarily angry with him or her, quit a job you really need because someone else got a promotion ahead of you, or take any number of actions that you can justify in the moment but seem really stupid quite soon afterward.

How do you know when you are in an emotional state? Think, are you sadder, more jealous, and moodier than you would ordinarily be, perhaps in reaction to something you heard or saw? Then do a reality check, take a breath, and determine that you are not going to allow yourself to make any decisions at that moment; instead, wait a few hours until you send that e-mail, or even take a day to respond, so that you can make sure you are *going to say what you really mean, and not something that's in reaction to what's been said.* Many times when you do this, it allows you to be in control of your emotions and gives you perspective on the angry situation. A cold, hard dose of reality always helps to dilute anger, especially when you realize that being angry is not going to change that reality.

Another anger-management technique starts the same way. It's hard, though: you have to catch anger fast. Anger builds momentum quickly, so if you don't take control of it immediately, it accelerates and gets out of hand. I have my own little dialogue with myself when I get angry. When someone pulls my strings, I think, This is *very* weak, and giving in to my anger is not going to make me feel better later. Depending on how angry I am, I might have to repeat this to myself a couple of times, or use "Monk for a Minute" (chapter 2) and the "Fifteen-Minute Technique" (chapter 5). I can get pretty pissed off, and I'm sure you can too.

If you are a person who is easily enraged, as I am, and as the thousands of kids at Brockton high were, you'll be throwing yourself a lifeline instead of throwing a punch if you learn to use anger-modification techniques.

The Shaolin monks teach us that anger and hatred have no other function than to destroy us. We can resolve to stop giving this enemy the opportunity to arise within us, as it has probably done for years.

SUFFERING (*DUKHA* IN BUDDHISM)

Want to suffer? According to Buddhists, there are three ways to do it:

SUFFERING OF PAIN. This includes all *physical and mental ailments and afflictions.*

SUFFERING OF CHANGE. This means that all *pleasure is temporary and eventually brings about further suffering and pain.* It is like scratching a mosquito bite, where the relief and satisfaction of scratching the bite are only temporary. Soon, it will itch like crazy. Another example would be eating a piece of rich cake when you are already full, then getting a stomachache. Or having an extramarital affair: you feel good, but it's temporary.

SUFFERING OF PERVASIVE CONDITIONING. This is *suffering when your mind is unenlightened.* As long as you don't seek to reach enlightenment, Buddhists believe, you'll never be at peace.

DO MONKS GET ANGRY?

Monks get angry at times—they are human—but the difference between most of them and us is that they are better at choosing what they do with the negative energy anger creates. They don't allow hate and rage to control them, because they have learned that allowing anger to take over in any situation is a form of weakness that should be replaced with understanding and compassion. Why weakness? Because anger is a lack of control that serves no purpose in life. All it does is cause misery that can lead to hatred—which is even worse.

If you have an argument with your partner, say, and your first inclination is to defend your position or otherwise lash out at him, before you say hateful or angry things, stop for a moment. As a thinking person, you have a *choice* to consider what you are going to say—not yell, hit, defend, or accuse—before you say it. Maybe the person you feel you're "up against" had a bad day at work, is sad about something, or is in his own funk and has taken it out on you. Maybe he picked the fight. Maybe it's in response to something you did in the past, that's coming out now—and more furiously—because he kept it locked away for so long.

From an Eastern perspective, it doesn't matter who started it, because if a problem that big is surfacing between two people, it's usually the dynamics between those people that make it so bad in the first place. The point is that when you come right down to it, no one wants to be thought of as the bad guy, which is why I came up with "The Asshole Theory" (see chapter 10, "You Can't Move On If You Can't Let Go") to help my students and others understand that most people are capable of being assholes only if that's something they've learned, either from their parents or from other authority figures. We react to situations and or words in whatever way we have been taught—and not in ways that reflect our capabilities as people who can change.

In trying to be patient or tolerant in any confrontational situation, you are in the fight against *your own impulses as much as you are in a fight with them*. And trying to beat anger is not easy, but it's essential. Studies at universities such as Duke and Stanford* have shown that anger is a major con-

---

*R.M. Sapolsky, L.M. Romero, and A.U. Munck "How Do Glucocorticoids Influence the Stress-Response? Integrating Permissive, Suppressive, Stimulatory, and Preparative Actions." *Endocrine Reviews* 21 (2000): 55.

tributor to disease and premature death. Rage, in particular, can damage the cardiovascular system, especially in men, and recent research suggests that repeated chronic temper loss can lead to a cardiac condition called "atrial fibrillation."* It's like watching one of those cartoons where the mercury goes up on a huge thermometer and eventually explodes: that's your heart under the pressure of rage.

Anger, hatred, and rage usually flare up when we feel provoked or hurt, and they cloud our minds and affect our judgment. Shaolin also teaches that anger and hatred cannot be overcome just by wishing they would go away, holding them in, or "waiting" for them to subside. Anger comes from frustration, lack of understanding, or feeling our ego has been bruised. These things make us want to protect ourselves and fight back. But fighting back usually just means adding to that simmering pot, and not doing anything can lead to feeling victimized or weak. The question is, how do you deal? The answer is, by thinking like a monk.

MONK FOR A MINUTE

This is the time to become Monk for a Minute.

When you begin to feel anger or rage take over every bit of common sense you have, think of how a Shaolin monk would deal with anger.

Picture yourself with a bald head, slippers, an orange robe, a pouch around your neck with

*Dr. Redford Williams, Duke University Medical Center.

some nasty herbs in it, and of course the ability to take on any ten large men physically. By the time you get through with this thought process, you'll most likely forget what the hell you were upset about. You have only a few seconds to put yourself in this mental state, or the anger will win. Then, everyone loses.

This actually works, but only if you focus on controlling your anger totally — not partially. You need to ask yourself at this point, "What am I doing, who am I going to inflict this pain on, besides myself, and do I really want to hurt these people/this person?"

Meditation: Anger is weak and evil, and there is no room for it in your life or anyone else's.

DIFFUSING ANGER

There are some specific ways to diffuse anger. In the morning, the monks do kung fu exercises and meditation that puts their minds and bodies in a state that allows them to be more at peace and balanced throughout their day. You can do your own kind of meditation when you feel yourself getting angry, just as it is happening, as part of the thought process, since most of us probably don't make time every morning to sit and meditate.

It might go something like this. Say you hear a rumor about yourself or someone you like (true or not). It makes you angry. You start to get upset either while you're alone or with the person who told you. Your pulse rate goes up, you pace, you gnash your teeth, you kill the messenger. At this point you've lost the fight with yourself. What if, instead, you heard the news, and where you might normally get agitated or fidgety, you let the angry response just roll off you?

Here's why that's important. The only reason you get angry is because you obviously care how other people perceive you or your friends. If you didn't care, a rumor wouldn't matter and it *would* just roll off you because it would have no meaning in the context of how you view yourself and your life.

Because I have always cared about what other people think of me (given my weak early self-esteem), this was always very difficult to do. It upset me terribly when someone would say something bad about me, and it was even more infuriating when it was someone I loved or had helped throughout his or her own life. It was like I was stabbed in the back. In that scenario, it was impossible for me to just let things "roll off my back," because at the time I was simply too insecure.

Now, I look at the person spreading the rumor from a whole new perspective. Instead of reacting with anger, I first say to myself, "This person is angry or upset with me for a reason, and whether it's legitimate or not, his feelings are real to him." This means that I examine what I did or might have done to contribute to his ill feelings toward me. This is what I call "diffusing myself." When this happens, I take the onus of being angry off myself, and ask why the other person is angry. Ninety-nine percent of the time the person is angry because I in some way let him down, or he thinks I did.

At this point, you have taken the anger off of yourself and not personalized it, which gives you the ability to approach the angry person in a compassionate way, and ask him what you did that upset him. In this way, the conflict has a real chance of being resolved because you chose to understand your anger—and his—and show compassion, rather than lose control, make things worse, and get absolutely nothing accomplished.

If you get angry, react without compassion, and your response gets back to the person who's upset with you, now he'll be even madder, and you won't speak to each other for the next twenty years. Or you might begin a war with the person: in your personal war, you pull all kinds of people in, and in turn they get angry at each other. Now your original problem has escalated to a full-on disaster involving many other people. It's much easier to deal with anger as it occurs, not let it absorb you, and thus head off further conflicts.

We get angry about rumors people spread about us, or someone we care about, because it makes us afraid that the rumor is going to affect our entire life, and the fact that people are saying bad things about us doesn't feel good. Remembering the truth and questioning why the person might be saying destructive things is a more constructive way of handling your feelings about the situation, because it may not even be about you (see "The Asshole Theory" in chapter 10).

In another way of looking at this, anger and hatred have already been created by someone else spreading the rumor, and your response just contributes to all that bad energy and doesn't make you feel any better, either. You're mad, you're sweating, your heart is racing . . . does this seem like a response that will make you feel better, even for a minute? You're still going to be angry later unless you break things down to their essence—why you are angry, why he is angry—and deal with it in the moment, instead of letting things simmer and get worse.

DO UNTO OTHERS

An emperor asked Confucius about benevolence.
Confucius said, "He who could practice five
things everywhere in the world would be
benevolent." "What five things?" the emperor
asked. Confucius said, "Courtesy, magnanimity,
sincerity, diligence, and clemency. He who is
courteous is not scorned, he who is
magnanimous wins the multitude, he who is
sincere is trusted by the people, he who is
diligent succeeds in all he undertakes,
and he who is clement can get
good service from the people."

LEAVING THREE SIDES OF THE NET OPEN

King Tang of Shang was the leader of the Shang tribe in ancient China and the founder of the Shang dynasty (sixteenth to eleventh centuries BCE). One day he went out on an excursion. Coming to a plain surrounded by mountains, he saw a man erecting a net enclosing a certain area to trap game inside, and muttering to himself from time to time. He was actually praying, "Let everything, no matter where it comes from, whether flying in the air or running on the ground, enter my net." Hearing these words, King Tang felt disturbed, and said to himself: "In this way, all the birds and beasts will be captured. Only a tyrant would do such a thing!"

Thereupon he had the hunter brought before him, and said to the man: "Make haste; and leave three sides of your net open; one side will be sufficient." He added an instruction that the hunter should pray as follows: "Those which want to go to the left, let them go to the left. Those which want to go to the right, go to the right. Those that want to fly high, let them fly high. Those which want to roam on the ground, let them roam on the ground. I only wish those that are doomed to die to be trapped in my net."

The story of how the hunter had been ordered to open his net on three sides spread around a river, where the rulers of the feudal states all came to admire the morality of King Tang of Shang. They said, "If King Tang of Shang's morality extends to birds and beasts, how much more fairly will he treat humans!" After this, forty of the feudal lords transferred their allegiance to King Tang of Shang, and Chinese lore tells us that to this day, King Tang is remembered as a truly compassionate soul.

Compassion is one of the most important lessons on the road to self-awareness, joy, and happiness, although it's one of the most difficult lessons to learn. Why? Because it's hard to see why we need to be compassionate to others when day to day, it's hard enough dealing with our own issues like changing behavior in our own lives that stop us from feeling happy and free, much less having to worry about some other person we don't even know! But this is a very limited perspective. This is looking too closely at the finger and not seeing the whole hand.

On the whole, we must first help ourselves before we can help others. This is obvious. If we're a mess in our own lives, how can we help others who are also a mess? But once we fix ourselves up, it's essential to help others, because only in helping others can we continue to help ourselves. I used this example before, but it's important to go back to it here. Imagine the planet as a small one-bedroom apartment, and it's stuffed to the brim with people. You might have found a nice corner to sleep in, but if a few other people don't have places to sleep, you can bet they're going to be pushing into you and trying to muscle in on your territory. We are all together on this planet, and we are all dealing with the same things: loss, love, anger, regret, bad childhoods, uncertain futures, the meaning of life, the definition of success—everything. And whether or not you accept the Buddhist belief that we are all one, you have to at least acknowledge that everything affects everything else. If 10 percent of the world's people are super rich and live in a stone castle, and the other 90 percent are super poor and have no food to eat, when they come storming in for your food, you can't be mad or angry at them. You've created the situation for yourself, by not realizing your responsibility as part of a collective whole that we call this planet.

Helping others means helping yourself. Having compassion for others means you know what they are going through. You feel their pain. You've walked in their shoes. You've been alone, hungry, or sad, and when you get yourself out of those funks, you want to help them because you understand that we are all in this together.

"Practicing" Compassion

I have learned that the Buddhist definition of compassion means to cultivate feelings of warmth and affection toward others, thereby improving our relationships. That means "practicing" compassion by wishing for others to be free of their suffering.

I say "practicing" compassion because many people do not realize that it is in fact a practice, something to work at. It is a difficult process for us as individuals, particularly in this culture. We are not monks: our lives aren't lived for the sole purpose of improving the lives of others, thereby improving our own—which they would consider crucial to the path of enlightenment. Instead, our lives are often centered on creating wealth, which in turn creates greed and detachment from other humans. Ironically, the very pursuit of what we sometimes think would make us happier—riches, fame, nice possessions—is the very thing that creates unhappiness and loneliness, because it is alienating.

When we are attached only to doing things for ourselves, it will only be a matter of time before we self-destruct. How much can one give oneself or serve oneself? Self-serving people lead very lonely lives, particularly if their energies are poured into acquiring wealth and not sharing it. People will be all around them because they want some of that wealth, or a favor, and not because they care or like the person. It is very hard for most people to give you something—compassion, generosity—that you are not willing to give yourself. A self-centered way of living may well lead to your waking up one day and finding no one else is there but you.

We live in a world that forces us to constantly fear for our survival. Therefore, it is difficult sometimes to live our lives with the kind of compassion defined by Shaolin, especially if we don't see the practical application of why we should. So the big questions are, how and why should we incorporate compassion into each part of our lives, especially when it does not fit with the governing mentality of our culture? If you're nice to someone unnecessarily, and not because you want something from them, won't that make you weak or vulnerable? you might wonder. Not if you're not attached to how the person is going to respond, it won't.

COMPASSION WITHOUT ATTACHMENT

There are some hidden dangers associated with compassion, the largest of which, say the Buddhists, is making the mistake of intertwining it with attachment. This is when you have a relationship, whether it's romantic or platonic, that relies on a kind of control, such as when you love someone so that he or she will love you back. So maybe you're being compassionate to get something in return, but relationships based on this alone are dangerous because they lack an understanding of what it means to be truly loving toward someone else. They also set us up for disappointment.

As we meet someone that we would like to have as a friend, we begin the "getting to know you" process. We have the tendency to get attached emotionally as we become closer to the person. This is when the danger begins, because once we feel attached because we have given of ourselves, then we begin to *expect* the person we are emotionally giving toward to react a certain way right back at us. If she doesn't, we get angry or hurt and sometimes feel victimized, because we now perceive her response to be a betrayal of our compassion and trust. Suddenly, we start to act differently toward her, and by now we've begun, unintentionally, a relationship based on attachment, not love and compassion.

Most of us have made this mistake at one time or another. Buddhists believe that all humans deserve to be free of suffering, and deserve to be happy, no matter where they come from. If we too can adopt this way of thinking, we begin to see that we are all the same from a fundamental point of view, and that it doesn't matter what color someone's skin is, or how much money he or she has. Each of us should be shown compassion.

If you treat all people like this, from the derelict on the subway, to the bitchy secretary outside the meeting you're late for, to an arrogant coworker or a rude salesperson, then it becomes easier to avoid basing your most important relationships on attachment.

Buddhists would say that if a person is truly compassionate, he or she will treat his or her friends and enemies exactly the same, because we all have the same basic rights as humans. This sounds a little crazy, I know, but this Buddhist analysis is different from a Western way of thinking precisely because it doesn't rely on "love" as it's taught in this society, where we "need" another person to give us love or compassion back when we put it out there to someone else. Buddhists would argue that truly compassionate relationships are much more substantial than love based on attachment, since they do not have any expectation of getting something in return.

This type of selfless compassion or nonattachment (a good deed without a purpose or a motive) gets you to a place where you can practice what the Buddhists call *wu-wei*. *Wu-wei*, translated literally, means "nonaction," but not in the conventional sense of laziness or apathy. Instead, *wu-wei* suggests an action conducted from a place of selflessness.* When you have compassion for someone you love, then it is wu-wei of you to relate to the loved one in such a way without expecting him or her to respond in any particular fashion—

*Master Sheng-yen, *Catching a Feather on a Fan,* Element Books, Great Britain, pp. 123–124.

particularly not with any kind of gratitude. This is really hard to do, and creates disappointment in our lives when we don't get back what we think we should.

It is a human quality to get attached to the people we are compassionate to, and their response or nonresponse to our kindness. This is one reason why many people don't get close to others. Many who choose to live with this kind of forced detachment are not necessarily bad people or people who don't have the ability to show compassion. Instead, they are usually people who are afraid to show others kindness because they have been so disappointed and hurt in the past in their efforts to get close to someone.

THE BEATEN DOG

Sometimes it is difficult to imagine true compassion without attachment. Once, I was going into the grocery store and saw a dog tied to a pole outside the store. The poor animal had wrapped himself around the pole so many times that he was hurting himself. I felt really bad for the dog because I knew he was in pain. I didn't, however, know the dog; he wasn't mine, so I wasn't attached to his pain as I might have been if he had been mine. When I went over to untangle the animal, I did not think about what would happen to him next, or whether this happened to him every day.

Similarly, when you see someone beating a dog, and it breaks your heart, it does not make you sad because you love the animal—it's not even yours—but it makes you feel terrible because on some level you recognize that like you, the dog has a right not to suffer in life or be beaten. Buddhists believe that you share a sense of humanity with the dog, and if you can think of the commonality of experience between all things that live and breathe, then the monks would say you have developed a greater understanding of the true nature of compassion.

Whether you've ever seen a dog beaten or a person you love hurt, there is a simple but effective way of thinking about what real compassion is for you. When you are not surrounded by noise, the demands of work, or your kids asking you for homework help, take a few quiet moments to imagine a person, any person, suffering. Or pick a dog, or a cow, or something else that is alive. The person or animal might be beaten, or hit by a car and in pain, or undergoing serious surgery in the hospital, all of which we might assume to be painful situations.

Think about how terrible he or she must be feeling; then turn your mind to how *you* would feel if you were in the same situation, and how lousy it would be to be hurt or beaten up or afraid to die on an operating table. Relating the person or animal's experience to your own creates the kind of commonality of experience that Buddhists believe allows us to connect our experiences to others' in ways we couldn't before, and by doing this we can see how similar all our situations are, which will in turn help us be more compassionate. Even though the scenario you are imagining might be fictional, you will probably find that it *feels* real, if you're really focused. If you were suffering greatly, wouldn't it be a great and profound joy to have someone help you—with no feelings of expecting something in return, but simply because the person cares, and knows what you're going through, or knows that we all go through difficult times?

Now switch the scenario. If you could help the sufferer out of his or her situation, would you?

COMPASSION FOR THE LONG HAUL

Buddhists, like Confucius, believe that what we do in this life carries on to eternity, and having studied Shaolin for many years I have come to believe the same. I ask myself every day what I will have left behind that will carry on to eternity, and once in a while I get a clear answer.

When I was a chief instructor of kung fu in Concord, New Hampshire, one of my students, Joe, a high-spirited sixteen-year-old and a very good martial artist, was in an almost fatal car accident. He was in intensive care and could not be visited by anyone but his immediate family. Every day I called, and all I was told was that in order to save Joe's life there had to be a very serious brain operation performed. Sadder still, they didn't know if he would survive it. This was devastating; I was very close to Joe.

Some time after the operation I received a call from his parents, who told me that Joe had survived the surgery, but that Joe would have to get out of bed and start walking around to jump-start his brain, or he would die. Thus far he had not moved, and he didn't seem too keen on doing so. His parents said that Joe, depressed after the ordeal, refused to get out of bed and didn't have a desire to be in any more pain than he already was. He routinely told everyone, including his parents, to leave him alone.

As a last resort, they asked me if I would go up and see him. This was the easy part for me. It took little compassion to do this. Where the real test came in was when I saw him. There he lay with his head completely covered with bandages, and many tubes and things hooked into his body. It made me sick: all I could think about was this high-spirited, high-kicking kung fu kid lying there looking as if he wanted to die.

This is where having compassion and being attached

kicked in. I felt so bad for Joe: he said that he just wanted to lie in bed, and as he was already in a lot of pain, the thought of having to get out of bed only represented more pain to him. All I wanted to do was to sit beside him and try to make him happy. Why, I reasoned with myself, did I have to get him out of bed, which would give him more pain, even though this was the only way he would walk again?

I had to somehow separate the attachment I felt for him from the ability to do what was necessary—which was actually compassionate, even if it was hard to do. This was obviously a lot different from the dog that was strangling himself being wrapped around a pole. I realized, for the very first time, that I would go the limit on practicing what I preached. The compassion part was easy; the nonattachment part seemed impossible.

I leaned over and whispered into Joe's ear, "I know that you got in a bad accident, and you're in a lot of pain, but if you don't get out of that fucking bed, I will show you what pain really is. And you know I can." I don't know where it came from—it was terrible: the kid was half dead—but it worked. Joe smiled, got up that very moment, put his arm around a nurse and me, and started to walk. He took only a few steps, and it took both of us to balance him so that he could do that. But each and every day for weeks, I came to the hospital room and walked with Joe, watching him cry out with pain.

I can't tell you how many times I wanted to let him sit down, how bad I felt when he would ask me to "please stop" because it was too painful for him. But I am glad that I made him continue: it was that fighting that kept him alive.

Joe survived and has gone on to live a normal life. The huge scar never went away, and he has had some struggles, but he has no permanent brain damage. This was my ultimate test of practicing compassion without attachment.

I recently heard Joe was back in Concord and was working for an old student of mine. I immediately went to see him, figuring I'd exorcise the old demons if I had a chance to see with my own eyes that he had turned out all right many years later. Joe had made it: he looked strong and he was smiling.

A Shaolin monk would say that the desire to end worldly suffering works on a local, personal basis, because by showing compassion to another (in the case of Joe, helping him get through his suffering) I helped myself. My experience with Joe taught me about the "right" kind of compassion.

My Friend Vinnie

The right kind of compassion comes in many forms, but you know it when you see it. One of the most important people in my life had this right understanding of compassion, but I didn't know it at first. I met Vinnie Vecchioni, my high school boxing coach, the day after the fight where I got my ass kicked at fifteen. He was a small, rugged-looking man with big forearms and a gruff personality. And he saved my life.

When I tell people today who know about boxing that I fought out of the Rocky Marciano Gym—the place the character in *Rocky* was named for—they are always awed. But it was a shit hole. A lot of great boxers came out of that place, but it was Vinnie Vecchioni who made people throw prizewinning uppercuts, not the dingy gym with the famous name. You had to walk through a bar—one of those nasty joints that smell like stale cigarettes and gin—to get to the gym.

I made my way past drunks and a few wise guys, eyeing the grimy walls in dim light that seeped through dirty windows. Holding my nose, I got to the gym, and saw Vinnie, flanked by heavy bags and spartan equipment. "I wanna fight," I said. Vinnie eyed my cut-up face. "I need some help though," I said, softer now.

"Show up tomorrow," he said.

And that was it. That's how it started. I couldn't wait to get my gloves that first day, but Vinnie wasn't giving me any. I sulked; I got wraps and bag gloves, a mouthpiece, and an athletic supporter. Not that I needed any of the protective gear for a long time. Vinnie had me practicing and learning the sport for six months before I ever got in the ring.

Vinnie could have been a monk: he knew I badly wanted to be in that ring, but he wouldn't let me go in because he instinctively knew that I was doing it for all the wrong reasons. I was like the disciple who wanted to learn the kung fu moves, but instead, the master told him to go and get some more water, or go clean the grounds and *then* go and stand in his horse stance for an hour. I didn't realize I was starting my Shaolin training in that old boxing gym, but I was.

I boxed and I ran: seven days a week, four hours a day. At night I would stagger home and fall into bed, and my mother never said anything, just that I had to go to school and graduate. Every day I'd come in, Vinnie would say just one word: "Go." And that meant I had to run two miles at least. I hated running. I worked the speed bag, then the heavy bag, and then shadowboxed. I couldn't wait to get in the ring, but when I did, I was scared to death, just like when I tried out for football. All I could see was big gloves coming at my face.

While Vinnie was the one who started me boxing, ironically, he was also the one who ended my career before it really began. For my first fight, they paired me up with an experienced boxer who had been fighting for five or six years. Before we went into the ring, we sat together and suited up, talking as we went. He told me how many fights he had won, compared to my 0–0 record, and I began to be afraid. I was going to get killed, it became clear. In the ring, the guy came at me and whacked me in the face once; but I got so mad that I easily beat the hell out of him.

The next day, I was all swagger. I skipped school, proud as hell that I had won my first fight, and went to tell Vinnie I was going to quit school and turn pro. I thought I was going to be the next Rocky Marciano or Muhammad Ali.

Vinnie didn't say anything, but here was where he started practicing his kind of compassion; he just put on my gloves for me and laced them up, telling me to change up. Now, Vinnie used to spar with us once in a while when he was teaching us new skills, and this particular day he decided he was going to spar with me. I got into the ring, consumed with the thought that I was going to be the next heavyweight champion of the world.

Vinnie promptly beat me into next Tuesday. Then he threw me into his car, didn't even take my gloves off, and drove me to Brockton High School. By one ear, Vinnie dragged me into Principal Busalari's office. I was cut up and bleeding, dressed in a tank top and boxing shoes, and Busalari looked amused, if confused. "If Steven misses one more day of school," Vinnie said, "I wanna know about it." He turned to me. "You're not quitting school, and you're not gonna be a fighter." I felt my ears start to go red. "You're gonna graduate and make somethin' of yourself."

Vinnie was willing to kick the shit out of me himself to show me what kind of potential I had that I could not see: here was his compassion. "Look around you," he said one day after we'd finished sparring. "You're not like the rest of these kids here. You're different." I had no idea what he was talking about, since from my perception I looked the same, grew up in the same neighborhood, and knew that I needed to fight to survive. "You, Steven, are gonna make it," Vinnie continued. "But let me tell you something," Vinnie advised. "Never forget where you came from, because if it all gets taken away from you, the only ones who are gonna be there are the ones you started with."

I remember this because it's such a good metaphor for how you overcome challenges, and as important, how you choose to treat other people with compassion.

There are not enough pages in this book to tell you how much your life will improve and take on meaning if you spend a little time each and every day helping to improve the life of someone else, as Vinnie did for me. He showed me clearly that being compassionate is the biggest and the most lasting gift you can offer *yourself*, even though on the surface it more immediately, positively affects others.

Practicing compassion has saved many lives I have known, and changed others: the first one, with Vinnie's help, was my own. A master once said, "People will forget what you do for them; they will forget what you give them; but they will *never* forget how you make them feel."

LEARNING HOW TO LOVE

A discussion of compassion would not be complete without addressing its counterpart, love. While there are many different kinds of love, each of them is naturally intertwined with a need for compassion, but sometimes it takes us years to learn what love really is and how to navigate through it in a compassionate way.

I, for one, was a late bloomer in this regard.

My mother always said to me, "Stevie, you're a great son, you're a great brother, you're a great friend—but you're a *terrible* boyfriend." You know when your mother (who is supposed to love you above all else) tells you something as harsh as that, it must be true. She would see me go through girls like water. It got to a point where I wouldn't bring anyone home to meet her unless I liked the girl more than most, because I knew what I would have to hear. One time, I really dug this girl Jenny, so I brought her for a visit and left her alone for a while with my mom while I helped my sisters do some yard work. When I came back, we all talked and laughed for a bit, and then Jenny and I left. In the car, she turned to me and said, "Does your mother *like* you?"

I thought that was a funny question. "Yeah, why?" I asked.

"Because she told me to stay away from you. She said I'm a really nice girl, but for you I'm probably just the flavor of the week."

And that was that. I didn't get mad. I didn't even mind that much, because I knew it was true; I was an asshole, and I'd finally been called out.

Needless to say, I didn't bring another girl home for a long time after that. In fact, before I met my wife, Kelly, I went from one woman to the next. The problem was, I was looking for the wrong things based on what I had observed as a child, and what I thought I wanted at the time.

It took me many years to recover from my dad being a bad father and then leaving, and my mom remarrying: as a young person, I never had a true family support system; even though my sisters and mother did the best they could—and the best they knew how to considering what they had to go through—they also depended on me to take care of them emotionally, and I was very young. I had no one to depend on or turn to for myself, and often ended up feeling abandoned and alone. Abandonment is a terrible thing, and it can happen even when there are two parents in the home, because being physically "there" is not the same as being tuned in and loving.

This dynamic worked its way into everything in my life, including my relationships. Without a strong sense of who I was and what I wanted, I typically became attracted to girls who were a lot like me: usually the girl came from an abused background, needed support, and had low self-esteem. Many times she was beautiful, but because of her troubled past, unattainable emotionally. And because neither one of us knew how to love ourselves, how could we possibly love each other? We couldn't. I only felt fulfilled emotionally by a woman needing me, because this is what I had done for my mother and sisters. But that's not what real love is all about.

Real love is finding someone whom you want to be with every day, someone you want to share a life with, who makes you laugh, complements your strengths and weaknesses, but who is fundamentally independent from you. It is not about attachment, or working out dynamics from the past. In other words, she doesn't *need* you. She *chooses* to be with you. And vice versa: you don't *need* her to fill some void in your life—you choose her because you know what you want in life, and she is it. This is a very powerful bond as you can imagine, because it comes from a place of real self-worth and belief in yourself, your decisions, and your feelings.

Kelly was the first woman who did not need me, and I was floored. When I first met her, she seemed to be everything I thought I could never have. She was beautiful, grounded, and had a family that seemed to be close; they ate dinner together, talked to one another with respect, laughed a lot and had fun. She represented everything I *should have been* looking for.

At first I didn't know how to pursue her. She would always take her lunch break by the pool in the gym I was teaching at, and I'd stand around that pool like a *chuch* (Italian slang for a dummy), talking to one of my lower-ranking students and never getting up the nerve to talk to her. Then I figured I'd start working out by the pool, but that didn't get her attention either.

Finally, after much frustration—she would only smile at me, and I didn't know how to talk to her—I sent my secretary down with a note saying, "Will you marry me this weekend?" She sent a note back saying, "I'm a little busy this weekend: maybe some other time." That was all I needed. The next day, I was down there talking to her. I had never done anything like that before to get a woman's attention. I'd never had to, because I hadn't been looking for someone who was hard to impress.

I knew that Kelly did not fit the pattern of woman that I had gone out with in the past. How was she different? She had been raised differently than I: she had a more stable life, she was more balanced, she had self-confidence, she was intelligent and beautiful: all qualities I never thought I possessed.

By this time I was in my early thirties and was a studied behaviorist, but I still made mistakes with women no matter how many people I counseled otherwise about their matters of the heart. What I ultimately needed to succeed with Kelly was to stop bullshitting myself.

THE BULLSHIT DETECTOR

Take a look at the statements below, and finish the sentence "I am not happy with the partner I'm with because _____."

1. My partner gives all her/his time to the children and has nothing left for me.

2. My partner is always working and has no time for me.

3. My partner isn't interested in sex, and I have needs.

4. My partner doesn't have any interest in what goes on in my life.

5. My partner doesn't care how he/she looks and dresses, which is why I'm always looking at other people.

6. My partner never has any interest in going out with me alone and always wants to have other people around socially.

7. My partner doesn't work and expects me to bring in all the money.

8. My partner wants me to work, and I think I should be home taking care of the children. Or My partner doesn't want me to work because he or she thinks I should be home taking care of the children.

9. My in-laws suck.

You might feel that some or all of these things are true in your relationship: that's why it is time to assess its status and see how it can improve. This can happen only if you stop "bullshitting yourself" about your role in the relationship, because agreeing with any of the above descriptions is only one side of the story. What's your role in the unhappy situation? What have you done with your partner to improve it? How have you made it worse?

STOP BULLSHITTING YOURSELF

You will need to draw on some serious power here to stop bullshitting yourself and change the type of people you date and go out with. Lots of times, people tell themselves they can't make a relationship work, or haven't found the "right" person, because there is "just something missing." None of the partners they've been with seem quite right, so in a futile search for what they think is going to make them happy, people keep looking until they get discouraged by a world of possibilities. Or, they settle, choosing to be with someone who they know will never allow them to be happy.

Happiness, security, and support within true and honest love require that you "stop bullshitting yourself" about your patterns, dig down to what they are, and begin the work of changing them.

We have to ask ourselves if we've been fulfilled by our relationships in the past that did not work out. Why did we love those people? Maybe we gravitate toward those whom we feel safe with, but are not necessarily in love with. Or maybe they are people we know will not love us back the way we want to be loved, representing someone in our earlier life whom we wanted love from. Either way, these relationships are painful and unhealthy.

That you're no longer with any of these people (or are about to leave one of them) is pretty solid evidence that the relationships were not fulfilling in one way or another. We are creatures of habit and routine, so you have to be brutally honest with yourself. Is it more painful to examine this on your own today, or continue this destructive pattern for many more years to come?

FIFTEEN MINUTES OF HARD STUFF

It's funny how we know what we don't want in a man or woman, and what we will complain about each time we get into a new relationship— but oddly, we usually don't know what we _do_ want. When adults think like this, they're right back in an infantile stage of life: it's the conscious/unconscious saying, "I don't like this and it doesn't feel good, but I don't know how to get out of it." This is when you're consciously making decisions, but you don't know or use reason to understand why: e.g., someone who acts out in anger and hits, but does not know why he or she is doing so. Letting this emotional response run your life will leave you feeling like a hapless victim if you let it. No one can change this pattern but you.

Here's the rub: if you can say, "I have been through several relationships in my life and none of them seem to last," what questions should you ask yourself? How do you change this pattern? Start with these:

- What do I want? What is the ideal mate for me?

- Do I want someone who is overprotective?

- Do I want someone who is emotional and can talk to me about his or her feelings?

- Do I want someone who is extremely affectionate verbally and physically?

- Do I want someone who is involved in every aspect of my life? Does he or she want to have a family and raise children?

When you can answer the questions, try changing the word "want" to "have," and see what you come up with. When you feel clear in your answers, the people you meet and attract will start to seem different to you—because they will be different than what you're used to.

LOOKING AT THE ROOTS TO SAVE THE BRANCHES

How did your parents interact? How much positive input was given to and programmed into you by your parents? Were loyalty and trustworthiness important in your family? As you already know, mine was a mess.

Our programming is only as good as our programmers—our parents or whatever authority figure helped raise us. If you don't come from a loving, supportive, and emotionally stable family structure, than you have missed out on the kind of early training that Shaolin warrior monks go through in order to give themselves a solid foundation for the life they lead. To grow into reasonably functional adults in our own hectic world, the first and most important characteristic we must develop at a young age is our own sense of personal security, because from that we begin to grow in other ways.

Someone once said, "How can you take care of the second thing if you didn't take care of the first thing?" meaning that you can't have the good stuff later on, accepting and understanding what it is to have a secure, loving, and lasting relationship, if you don't first feel secure at the onset.

THE COMPASSIONATE PARENT

Practicing compassion with your children is sometimes very difficult, and requires special tools, particularly the ability to hear what they are *not* saying. Many times your children are more tuned in to your feelings and state of mind than others might be—sometimes even more than you! It has been said that young kids are like sponges, and they soak up all the information—positive and negative—around them with often alarming ability. In this case, it means that they *know* you are tired or not in a great mood, so although they would love to have your attention, they will leave you alone and not ask anything of you, or they'll bother you because you're always in that state.

If you are tired and don't want to do any activities with your child, it is tempting, I know, to figure that if they don't ask you for any attention, it means they don't want any. If this sounds familiar, you may already have convinced yourself that you have some sort of freakish "maintenance-free" child. Don't accept this. Your children need your time and compassion. The time you spend consumed by your own problems and issues—and leaving your children's emotional needs unfulfilled—will come back to haunt you in spades. From all the families I have worked with over the years, I've been able to recognize a pattern in kids whose parents are not actively compassionate with them.

It usually starts with a lack of respect paid to the parents, continues with a lack of self-control, and becomes worse when the child starts to physically challenge you and others. But he or she is expressing the very same qualities *you've* been showing him or her! These are clear signs that you are not fulfilling the child's emotional needs.

I saw an example of this recently in one of my martial arts studios. A dad and his son came into my office because the son wanted to meet me. The boy, who was nine years old and big for his age, was respectful and shy. He then started his lesson with other students while the father began to talk with me. He asked me if I could sum up briefly why schools are having so many problems with disconnected children today.

I told him I thought it was because kids are angry at the lack of nurturing and attention they are receiving from their parents, both of whom often work day and night, though of course they don't know how to express this other than acting out at school.

The father agreed, and walked out of the office. Just then I happened to look into the studio, and I saw the child getting very upset; he threw a tantrum, and the instructor was having difficulty handling him, so I went over. I learned that the boy suffered from separation anxiety, because he kept asking where his father was, and repeatedly said that his dad hadn't told him he was leaving the building.

I went outside to look for the father, and found him playing with his dog. I carefully told him that his son was very upset that he had left. The dad got mildly defensive and said, "I told him I was leaving." I knew for a fact that he hadn't, or the boy would not have been so hysterical. I then asked him if his son was doing well in school, but getting a response was like pulling teeth from a dragon. The boy, who had attention deficit disorder as well as other emotional problems, had been sent to many doctors and away for several weeks to camps that the father insisted "dealt" with these types of problems.

I'm sure you have already figured out what the problem was here: instead of trying to show compassion for his son by giving him love at home and teaching him self-discipline, and also combating the kid's fears of abandonment by visibly sticking around for his son's kung fu class, I guess it was more important to be out playing with his dog. When the son took the lesson, he would look over after he did a move for his dad's approval, and no one was there. Many, many children take that look, and no one is there for them, either.

What never ceases to amaze me is that these parents are always *asking for the answers*, yet they don't even see their own inattention and lack of compassion for their children as the problem. In the case of the boy and his father (and many situations, I am sure, in your own life), practicing compassion takes effort, because there are often going to be things you would rather do with your time and attention. But there are lives at stake here: your children's. Without being shown care and compassion, they will turn into adults who are disconnected from themselves, the people who love them, and the very world they live in.

RELATIONSHIPS ARE HARD WORK

There is no Shaolin philosophy for relationships or marriage: of course, monks do not have partners. However, there are some Shaolin monks that were once in committed relationships, but gave them up to dedicate their life to Buddha and to train in kung fu. But if a Shaolin monk were with a partner, you can rest assured he would use the same methods of focus, compassion, and discipline to make it work.

Relationships are hard. People are different. We want different things, think in different ways, and when you put two of us together, no matter how "perfect" we are for each other, there are going to be disagreements, and there is going to have to be a lot of compromise. Add to that the fact that we are constantly growing and changing—on our own and with our partners—and it becomes that much more important to keep communication lines open should problems arise.

There are only two things to do when this happens. The first is to go to a counselor, which many people do. The reason for this is that it's often difficult for partners to communicate openly what's bothering them in the relationship. Touchy issues like "You don't have sex with me anymore" or "You're never around" are almost always tied to deeper issues, and getting to the bottom of them (especially if you're living in the same house with your partner) might be easier if a third party is involved.

The other method, and the one I use with my wife, is simply to sit down and talk it though. Tell your partner that you know things haven't been too great, but you want to work them out. Your partner will almost always know exactly what you're talking about because he or she doesn't live in a vacuum, and when you're in a committed relationship, when something is affecting you, it's affecting both of you—unless your partner is in complete denial. If he or she *is* in denial, it's very important to remember not to get frustrated or angry. What's the point in that? You already learned from the last chapter that anger isn't going to get you anywhere. What you really need is focus.

If your partner gets frustrated because he or she is not ready to accept that something is wrong, it will take a very strong mind not to get angry or frustrated, but diplomatically explain where you're coming from. When you get through that part, it's helpful to suggest that each of you make a list of things that you think could improve the relationship. This doesn't have to be done on the spot; in fact, I recommend that you make the list separately and reschedule a time when the two of you will sit down and go over things again.

When you do exchange lists, it is very important not to take your partner's words too personally and get angry. This is where the Buddhist philosophy of compassion, but not attachment to the other person's point of view, can help support your negotiation. Without a doubt, what each of you will write will upset the other person. Because of this, you'll have to try not to get attached to what you're reading on your partner's paper. Refocus your energy on the process of exploring the problems and concerns, and keep reminding yourself that you and your partner are seeking a *solution, together*. Although you might think that some or most of what you read from the other person is bullshit, this is not important. What *is* important is that a condition in the relationship has bothered your partner enough to list it. Then you have the opportunity to work through the list, concern by concern, deciding what is most important to work on first and agreeing that your partner's concerns are important enough to address.

8

HOPE IS AN ACTION

**All war, hate and fear can be conquered if men
would act in a loving way toward each other.**

—Mo Tzu

WILLING NOTHING INTO SOMETHING BY DOING

There were several books written about the idea of hope by
Dr. Viktor Frankl, a psychologist who had been a prisoner in
one of Hitler's concentration camps. As a young man, he was
arrested with his new wife and family in Vienna, and taken to
a concentration camp in Bohemia. He was later transferred to
Auschwitz alone, forced to leave behind his beloved wife and
children, who were taken to another camp. During that hor-
rific experience, he conducted a study where he collected
data on other men who were at the camps, having the same
hardships as he was, living under the same terrible conditions. They had health problems, were terrified for their lives,

and missed their families. Dr. Frankl wondered why some lived and others died, since everyone in the camps suffered from the same negative and very challenging experiences.

After he was released, Frankl, who had kept the manuscript for his famous book, *Man's Search for Meaning,* his life work, sewn into the lining of his coat during his transfer to Auschwitz, reconstructed the book from memory. The Nazis forced him to get rid of the manuscript on his way to Auschwitz, and it was the writing of memories and pieces of the manuscript on tiny slips of contraband paper at the camp—in the hope that it would someday be published and help others learn about the power of hope itself—that kept him from succumbing to typhoid fever. When his camp was liberated in April 1945, Frankl returned to Vienna to find that all of his loved ones were dead. He proceeded to fight through his despair to address questions about why camp victims had been hopeful, survived, or succumbed, after which *Man's Search for Meaning* was published.

In the book, Frankl discusses in detail how all of the men who ended up surviving were the ones who continually reminded themselves that they had reasons to live: men who hoped to survive. This hope was usually driven by love or memories of love.

Frankl's theories about man's survival being based on love and hope had been read by nearly nine million people the world around by the time of his death in 1997. He helped people understand that pain, death, and suffering are natural dynamics of life, balanced only by a sense of hope.

The Shaolin don't fear death, but they do have hope. Every day they strive to rid the world of pain and misery. They train and pray to reach Buddhahood, or reach Buddha himself through prayer. Spending every day and night engaged in such a practice might seem ridiculous and without any guarantees to us, but at its core is the embodiment of hope. They believe all people are essentially good, but there are many things in the world they cannot control. So they don't say to themselves, "I am confident that I will be able to rid the world of misery." Instead, they do the best they can, and go after their goals with the hope that they will one day attain them.

HOPE VERSUS EXPECTATION

In our culture we put too much emphasis on hope, so we are usually disappointed when we expect something to happen and it doesn't go our way. This is not hope. This is expectation.

It's interesting that in the *American Heritage Dictionary*, another word for "hope" is "expect," but in everyday practice these are really two different things. Many Buddhist scholars caution against using expectation as a crutch in life, and warn about the dangers of doing so. Wang Ming, a Chinese master who lived in the sixth century CE, wrote a thoughtful poem called "Calming the Mind," which is partly about how attachment to outcomes, or anticipation and then disappointment, can deter the process of meditation. In it, he advises his disciples to "close down the orifices and shut down the six senses," in order that they might gain more clarity on the here and now, rather than expecting to feel anything.

"Anticipation and disappointment create attachment and greed," writes Master Sheng-yen, who teaches the works of Wang Ming and other Buddhist scholars as part of his meditation sessions. He continues,

> Once upon a time, when I was a young monk near Shanghai, I was with a group of boys who were so poor that we hardly ever had enough food. One day, an old monk of better means provided us with some additional

dishes. Amongst them was a plate of bean curd. It was such a rare treat that one boy set aside a small slice so that he could relish it later on. He nibbled a tiny bit every day. For three days he managed to spin it out. But then one of our teachers saw what was happening. He slapped the boy and threw away his bean curd. The teacher told him, "With this attitude, you will end up as a Hungry Ghost!"*

The moral of that story is bigger than making a piece of tofu last. In reality, the boy hoped he would never go hungry again, so he tried to savor the feeling of being full by eating his food slowly. He became attached to the idea. He didn't go out looking for food. He didn't work to get money for more food. He simply expected that things would work themselves out now that he had some bean curd.

When we expect something to happen, we set ourselves up for failure and disappointment. There are many things in life we cannot control, so what happens when we expect a new car for our birthday, and then our parents lose all their money and can't afford one? We get disappointed. When we expect someone to call and he or she doesn't, we get upset.

Many of us in the West have been conditioned to believe that if we are good people, if we are kind, help others, do what we think is right, then good things will happen to us. If we don't think that way, we at least think that if we do all of the above, then bad things won't happen to us. Or at least we "hope" they don't. But this is not how the universe works, no matter what religion you are. Disappointments will always occur. No matter how hard we try to prepare for them or

---

*Sheng-yen, *Catching a Feather on a Fan*, Great Britain, Element Books, p. 37.

"hope" otherwise, we just can't control everything, which is why expectation doesn't get us anywhere.

Hope is separate from this kind of attachment to an outcome. For example, if we are working toward buying our own car and hope we'll one day have enough money, and then our parents buy us one for our sixteenth birthday, we're overjoyed. We didn't expect that. But if they never buy us a car, it doesn't really matter because we are still focused on our goal of buying it ourselves. We are not attached to the outcome of the situation. It is not stopping us or elevating us in some artificial way. We still work every day with the hope of attaining our dream, just as a Shaolin monk would do. We don't get lazy and sluggish because we expect it will happen, and therefore we don't get disappointed when it doesn't. What is disappointment really, besides feeling let down by a person or situation that we had hoped would turn out differently—when we didn't necessarily *do* anything constructive to bring that outcome to pass?

Hearing about a sick individual, saying, "I hope that person is all right," and then forgetting about it is really an empty statement. You're not doing anything. It's not hope. It's a throwaway statement. You didn't wish him or her well in your mind. You didn't send a card. You're just saying words that have no real meaning for you, with a possible expectation that the person will get better one day, and if he or she doesn't, it doesn't really matter because you didn't care much in the first place.

Hope is an action, whether it's mental or physical. It has focus, direction, and purpose. If we hope that people devastated by a natural disaster will be all right, this usually entails going to church, praying for them, donating money, or in some way trying to help contribute to the success of the goal.

MY MOM, THE SHAOLIN WARRIOR

My mother, Carol, was the shining embodiment of hope. She worked hard throughout her life to achieve her goals, always hoped for the best, and was always optimistic when things didn't turn out her way, because she knew that she couldn't control everything in life. And what's more, she maintained this kind of Shaolin warrior mind-set throughout a very difficult life.

Carol never got along with her own mother, Concetta, who wanted to have her aborted while in pregnancy. But since Concetta was an Italian Catholic, having an abortion was strictly prohibited, so in order to get rid of the baby, Concetta wrecked her car into a tree one night. As a consequence, my mother was born with broken bones, four fingers on one hand, and a multitude of other deformities. She spent much of her childhood at St. Giles Catholic Hospital, where she underwent many surgeries to correct her physical problems.

When she was nearly nine, Carol was admitted for yet another operation, after an earlier operation to correct her polio-stricken legs went badly, resulting in a terrible case of gangrene. She went into the operating room, got anesthetized, and when she woke up, her legs were gone. Shocked, terrified, and confused, she had nowhere to turn, and certainly nothing left to stand on. The hospital had chosen to cut her legs off from the knees down without telling her. "Maybe that was better," she said years later. "I don't know."

Years of rehabilitation followed. My grandfather, John DeMasco, or "John the Junkman," had a scrap metal business, which paid for my mother's hospital care. It was an easy solution for him, given Concetta's disdain for my mother. Certainly it was not an easy life for Carol, whose every waking moment was an emotional and physical struggle.

Mom was brought up by nuns, who called her by her much-hated middle name, Gertrude, and for a time after her operations, she had little faith in herself or a God who could make her disabled. "My legs were gone, and I just didn't want to get out of bed," she once told me. Then this nasty nun came up to her and said, "You know what, Gertie? You can just sit on that bed and feel sorry for yourself, or you can get up and walk. If you don't, you'll be in that bed for the rest of your life."

She got up. So why did my mother survive so well, in spite of all her hardships? How did hope serve her? How was it that she learned to walk with two wooden legs as well as people with real ones, and proved those doctors wrong who said she would never drive a car or have children (they assured Carol that her children would be deformed if she tried to have any, but she did anyway; my sisters and I have all ten fingers and toes).

If you were a nonreligious person, you would say that the nun's direct words were the turning point for my mom, and that through sheer determination she overcame her obstacles. She realized that she could sit in bed and simply wait to die, or she could be hopeful that things would get better, get up, teach herself to walk with prosthetic legs, and by doing that make her dream of "getting better" a reality.

If you are a religious person, you might say my mom was Catholic and therefore her hope and faith in God got her through. The monks, by contrast, would say that Gertie's accepting her reality was a result of Buddhist destiny, and she was simply living into hers.

According to Shaolin, what happened to my mom was predestined: she had come back to life for the second, or hundredth, or thousandth time from her last lives, as a person who would lose her legs so that later in her life she could, in some small way, inspire and help other people and lessen their misery. Had she been afraid to die, and had no hope, she likely would have died, because once you're in that frame of mind, it can lead to more pain and suffering, depression, health problems, and then death.

In the end, Mom ended up driving a car, having five children, raising her family, and becoming the local director of Head Start, a federal program that assists millions of families in need. She *literally* saved lives, and was loved and respected by thousands of people.

Carol was ironic and funny in how she looked at life's potholes. She once told me a story about a time she was at Grand Central Station, waiting for a train. My mom was beautiful, and there were always guys hitting on her. That day it was a handsome soldier, and she was flirting with him, too. Because she was wearing one of the long dresses women wore at the time, you couldn't even tell she had wooden legs from the knee down, even though back then, the prosthesis was really crude, and the person's stump would be stuck right to the leg.

Usually, Carol walked really well in her fake legs, but this time as she was coming down the stairs, the strap holding one of her legs on broke. Well, when that leg fell off and rolled down the stairs, most people would have been mortified, but not Carol. The soldier sputtered, asking if he could do anything for her. Propping herself up against the banister, she looked the poor man—who by this time was white in the face—dead in the eye and said drily, "Yeah, go get my leg." He did. "Now give me your belt," she demanded. The embarrassed soldier handed it over; my mom took it, hobbled to the ladies' room, and used it to tie her leg back on.

When she came out, the guy was gone. I can bet you she

never said to herself: "Gee, I hope I get another date." She knew that because of her inner and outer beauty, and positive attitude, she would. I still have my mother's legs. She always told me when she died she wouldn't need her legs, because God would be giving her legs in heaven.

Carol never felt sorry for herself. She was a caregiver: her priority was raising her children and helping others. So far as I could tell, my mother never hoped for legs; she simply realized she no longer had them, and that was that. She never hoped for wealth, realizing in her adult life that she was likely to be poor, and stay poor. Carol was the perfect embodiment of a modern day Shaolin warrior monk. She was strong, she was humble, and she never wanted anything for herself. She lived in the present and never expected anything. Her hope had direction and focus. She knew what she wanted—to give others hope in their times of need, much as she had been given hope—and she achieved that goal throughout her life.

In following her Buddhist destiny, what my mom did was not much different from how a Shaolin monk—even one with physical disabilities or other limitations—would be expected to live in the world. There were many warrior monks who were blind, and managed to be great teachers of Buddhist philosophy and the martial arts in spite of their handicap. Try to sneak up on a blind Shaolin monk: I wouldn't advise it.

Other monks had lost parts of their bodies in accidents, and were great warriors still, because there is a saying in Shaolin that when you lose the right arm, the left one becomes stronger. If you lose your legs, your arms become faster and stronger. If you lose both your arms and your legs, your *mind* becomes your sharpest weapon and tool, because your focus is on sharing great wisdom with others.

Anything can be accomplished with great faith and discipline, say the monks, which takes us back to faith alone needing a companion, action, in order to make hope a positive use of one's emotional energy in life.

WHERE THERE'S A WILL, THERE'S A WAY

One evening some years ago, the phone rang, and it was my mom: she'd received a call from a woman who had heard about her struggles in life, her work with Head Start, and how she was a double amputee.

This woman had a son, Thomas, who was eleven years old and had recently been hit by a truck, which dragged him over eighty feet. He was fortunate to be alive. The woman also told my mom that her son had been a star baseball player, whose life was entirely focused on the game. The doctors told Thomas that he was going to lose one of his legs, and he was devastated, as any person would be, never mind an eleven-year-old athlete.

Thomas became depressed and silent, refusing to talk to anyone since he had received the news about losing his leg. He wouldn't even talk to his parents, which made them terribly sad and frustrated. For weeks they had tried to get him to speak, with no success. Finally, through some health care workers in their community, the mother got wind of Carol and her particular gifts for working with difficult family situations, and reached out for help. Would Carol talk to her boy? she pleaded. My mother had read of the tragedy in the local paper but did not know the child. Still, she told the distraught mother she would try to talk with Thomas.

Mom asked me to go with her for company. When we went in to see Thomas, he watched my mom every step of the way. He looked angry, and when she came to his bed, Thomas looked right at her crutches, which she used daily later in life.

He could not see that she had wooden legs, because of her long dress and smooth way of walking. We tried for several minutes to get Thomas to say something, but he would not. It seemed like an hour to me: I don't know about my mom, but I was extremely uncomfortable.

Carol looked at me and said, "Stevie, wait outside for a few minutes. I want to talk to him alone." Then she handed me her crutches. I waited outside for over half an hour, expecting my mother to come out with a disappointed look on her face. However, she did what very few could do, but what she knew best from her own life experience: I believe she offered Thomas hope that he, like her, would be okay with one leg instead of two. She didn't hope the kid would talk to her: whether he did or he didn't, she would try to help him.

Thomas had a smile on his face as though the accident had never happened. My mom then proceeded to tell me that he was going to be operated on after all, and that Thomas accepted that he was going to get an artificial leg. As she spoke these words in front of him, the boy did not flinch or look otherwise upset. In fact, my mother cheerfully said that the kid couldn't wait to get his prosthesis fitted, and start training for baseball again with his new leg. I couldn't respond: I was in a state of shock.

When we left the hospital, I asked my mom what she had said to him. She responded simply, "Not much . . . he's a nice boy," smiled, and kept walking. To this day, I still don't know what she said. All I know is what she *did*: she didn't hope for any outcome to the situation, but instead used her energy to give hope to Thomas that he could learn to walk and function just as well as Carol. Like my mother, Shaolin monks don't want anything for themselves: they exist solely to improve the quality of life for others.

Carol DeMasco "got it." Just as an old Shaolin master once

said, "Give hope to others and you will never need it," Carol overcame adversity in her life by looking past her disabilities, embracing what she had and what she didn't, and choosing to pass hope on to others rather than "expect"—there's that word again—things in her life to be different.

There were Shaolin warrior monks who used their fighting skills to give others hope and protection, and there were Buddhist monks who spent much of their time praying to Buddha for things they would like to see happen. Personally, in my experience, praying alone isn't enough unless it is backed by action. This, to me, is the difference between a Buddhist and a Shaolin Buddhist monk: in other words, a person who prays versus a person who prays *and* does.

For some, faith and prayer alone are enough to get through the perils of life, and while I am not suggesting that anyone give up his or her faith, I have found that my faith in God requires a supplement to help me get through the days, survive the worst ones, and come out fighting for myself and for the lives of others. When I would ask my mom why God would allow so many bad things to happen to us and other kids in the projects, she would respond, "Stevie, God helps those who help themselves."

Hope is an integral part of a successful, happy life, but it is not a cure-all. Only through hope can you develop and maintain the desire to take the path toward whatever you consider success, by rooting out fear, pain, and suffering, and *using the energy you decide to spend on hope to constructively work towards what you want for yourself and others.*

TRUE POWER COMES FROM WITHIN

In the East, the dragon represents ultimate power. To attain ultimate power, one must develop inner strength and refrain from taking direct action: Be observant, think carefully, ponder and contemplate. Consult with those wiser and more knowledgeable than yourself. Cultivate and develop noble attitudes, firmness, strength, moderation, and justice. This, say the Chinese, is true power.

Many times in life we feel as if there is a set of rules determined by society that we have to play by, and sometimes they make us feel powerless. What are life's "rules," and who makes them? Worse, why do we have to follow them? I bet you've wondered this before, just as I did for many years, when your parents prevented you from doing something, you didn't get treated like everyone else, or you felt mistreated by people with more power than you. The seemingly arbitrary rules piss all of us off a little because our inability to change them makes us feel weak. Life's rules are just big thorns to us, and they take away our sense of power. And everyone wants power.

For different people, power means different things:

- To a businessperson, it might mean having or making more money.

- To a business manager, it might mean more people to manage.

- To a mom, it might mean more control over her children.

- To a young child, it might mean more toys.

- To older children, it might mean more independence.

- To a politician, it might mean a higher position in government.

- To a criminal, it might mean more acts of crime to commit.

- To a world leader, it might be more worlds to lead.

For me and for other kids who grew up like me, having power meant no more welfare lines, not going to bed hungry, and having nice clothes. It meant no one beating me up or abusing me anymore. I would look for ways to obtain power, and the obvious options where I came from were gangs, drugs, guns, and all the usual street crimes. Power, to the more privileged classes, means access to education for the purpose of securing a respected position in society, giving status.

No matter whether you're a cabdriver dominating an entire block of traffic, the CEO of a Fortune 500 company deciding what companies you are going to take over, the leader of a country at war deciding whom you are going to bomb, or a gang leader deciding which rival gang leader you are going to shoot, the motivations are all the same: *obtaining power*.

That's because nobody—nobody—wants to be seen as weak. Especially someone like me, a kid from the inner city. And to fight this perception of weakness, many of us will do all we can to appear powerful—not unlike different animals that puff themselves up when threatened to seem bigger than they are to enemies. In my early life, it was simple: I thought that if I could learn to fight, then start the fights, then win them, I'd have the most power. The rules wouldn't matter, because *I'd* be making the rules.

Our confusion about who makes the rules, who's powerful in our lives, and why we have to follow their rules goes back to childhood. I started wanting to know who made the rules when I was six years old. At a time when I should have been thinking of Play-Doh, crayons, and G.I. Joes, I tried to imagine what it would be like to have the same life as all those other kids who looked as if they were so much happier than I. Why was I different? They had nice clothes and nice toys, appeared to have families that loved one another, went on vacations to Disneyland together, and had lots of food.

But I was poor. I spent the time I wasn't in elementary school waiting on welfare lines for food and clothing, which my mother could not afford. Some days, all we had to eat was saltines and milk, which she mashed up in a paper cup for me. Carol, my mom, made really bad choices in men. The first one was marrying my dad, Al, a demented guy who as I have mentioned beat her and sexually abused me. Because he had what I thought was power—he was bigger, stronger, angrier—I followed his rules.

It turned out that that meant I had no physical prowess, no control, and little hope for things to be different. On top of that, I was a puny kid who got beat up a lot. In short, I had no power. The feeling was awful, and it grew worse the older I got. I didn't realize I needed to make my own rules.

POWER IN THE STREETS

I was not unique in being frustrated by the rules. About ten years ago, I was recruiting gang members and other street kids to join my martial arts and mentoring program. Here I was, a white guy in the ghetto of New Haven with twenty or more tough boys and girls around me. I was unarmed: when I reach out to inner-city kids, I don't bring any backup—no cops, no guns—nothing that would make the kids feel threatened or give them another reason not to trust me.

In the middle of the talk, when I was sharing what I do with martial arts and what they could expect if they came to join the program, one of the boys spoke up loudly, challenging me. For some reason, he didn't like what I saying, or my mannerisms, who knows? He looked at me angrily, then said, "Fuck you and this kung fu shit: all I need is *this*." Then he stepped forward and got in my face while reaching into his coat pocket.

I noticed right from the beginning that many of the kids were watching him to see what his reaction to me would be. Up until that point, he had the usual blank hard-core stare that all street kids learn to put on to protect themselves.

Here is an example of two *very* different types of power. He was trying to impress his friends with his toughness and his gun, and I was trying to win over a bunch of street kids. We were face-to-face; usually I don't let anyone get that close to me, but I did this time because if he was going to pull a gun on me, I had a better chance of disarming him at close range.

I didn't respond for about fifteen seconds, and I didn't attempt to stare him down, but instead kept looking at the other kids. I knew I could take him before he could shoot me, but I wasn't confident that someone else wouldn't get shot. Knowing his sense of power would not be upset if I challenged him to something he thought he could do better than I, I knew what my next step had to be.

Finally I looked at him. "I'll tell you what. I'll make you a deal. If you can get to what you have in your pocket before I get you, you can shoot me. If you can't," I said with a stupid smile on my face, "you have to take my kung fu class."

Well, he didn't know what to do. I appeared too ridiculous to shoot, which is what I was betting on, and that because of this he would hesitate to pull the gun. At that point he stepped back, took his hand out of his pocket, and said, "Fuck you man, you are fucking crazy."

At that point I knew I had won, without threatening his position of power.

The next day, and several times after that, along with some of the other kids who were interested, he came to my studio and took my class. His sense of power had not been upset by my challenge, and he saw that he wouldn't be weak if he let me try to teach him something. This was Shaolin at its best because while my life was definitely at risk, instead of acting with my ego and my power, where someone—even I—could have been hurt or killed, I gave up some control and offered him a compromise during the conflict, and he accepted.

He was not entirely powerful, nor was he totally weak, and neither was I. The kid got a chance to do something good for himself out of the situation instead of shooting me, which would have been far less powerful and much more damaging to his life, because any idiot can shoot a gun; and I got a chance to help him see that not everything had to be about violence—that he could still be powerful and not have to shoot anyone. Unfortunately, he was shot a week later in a gang war and died. I was really sad: I liked him, and I know that after we got past our initial squaring off about power, he liked me back.

This story, like so many others I have been a part of, just reinforces what the Shaolin warrior monks believe, which is that everyone is basically good and all people want to do good things: they just need be shown the right way. But sometimes it is too late.

CHANGING YOUR PERSPECTIVE ON POWER

Early in my martial arts training, I figured if I could become really good at kung fu, I would be powerful, and this pursuit couldn't possibly hurt anyone but me, physically, because I was doing it for me. Chinese philosophy says that you train for body and mind, but I was training to punch faster than anybody else, since I thought speed would give me the most power. But the more I worked at it, the less kung fu I was able to learn. It was very frustrating. I would go to Grand Master Fu, one of my early teachers, and ask him questions. "Sei fu," I'd say, "my right leg is too stiff, and it won't stretch far enough. How can I get more flexible?"

He would look at me flatly and say nothing. When I pressed him, he would sometimes glare at me, then mutter in broken English, "Just work harder." Surely, I thought to myself, this can't be the elusive "secret" of the Eastern martial arts. Fully fueled by my ego, I soon quit Fu's lessons, thinking I would never get the power I sought that way.

Master Yon Lee, my next teacher, had a similar approach to helping me learn the discipline. When I told him that it seemed like the more I stretched, the tighter I got, his response was "Just stretch more." Master Lee also had conditions: He wouldn't teach me the Shaolin forms unless I was willing to learn Chinese medicine and cooking. I would take three lessons in one day: first martial arts for an hour, then a medicine class where I learned to mix up all sorts of foul Chinese herbs into poultices, and finally an hour of cooking. Practicing the breath control so integral to a form like "Tiger," where concentrating on balance and springing from one point to another like the big cat are key, then slaving over a hot stove, was not my idea of fun. My days spent in the kwoon were confusing, sweaty, exhausting, and worst of all, smelly.

"I don't want to do medicine or cook," I told him. "I spent years cooking for my mother, sisters, and stepfather because Mom couldn't even make toast!" I felt I'd done enough of that. Sei Fu Lee eyed me, handing over a mortar and pestle. He didn't seem mad. Nor was his resolve to have me prepare food and herbal remedies deterred in the least. "Grind," he said gruffly, indicating I had no choice in the matter. I rolled my eyes and obeyed, adding herbs to the medicinal mixture he wanted me to concoct.

There I was, dragging myself twice a week into Boston's Chinatown from Brockton for a martial arts lesson, and this guy was asking me to be a mad scientist, of all things. I didn't want to believe that all these seemingly peripheral activities were part of the spirit—and correct and pure practice—of martial arts.

We didn't like each other, Master Lee and I. But he put up with me out of respect for a mutual friend, who'd introduced us. I stayed because I began to learn a great deal from him, and he ended up using the medicine I was resisting to heal me. Master Lee gave me what no orthopedic surgeon had been able to: fifteen years' use of my knees, which by this time were damaged from sports and martial arts.

The Chinese herbal compresses we made, which I mixed

and Lee applied, were as hot as hell, and sometimes hotter. But they worked. I would leave a session far less creaky than I had entered: my knees were healing, just like my soul. It began to occur to me that herbs were indeed part of the Chinese "secret" I was so desperate to figure out, and that maybe I was fighting for the wrong kind of power. My desperation was just like a lot of people's: I wanted to be the strongest, fastest, and best fighter going, as many of us want to make more money, have nicer things, be the top salesperson in our office, or win recognition for being great at a skill. But the reality was, my impatience made me weaker, and the small glimpses I got of how much stronger I was mentally and physically when I followed the master's program—instead of my own—taught me to differentiate between what real power is, and what it isn't.

A few years in, I could cook a mean Peking duck and heal people. I learned how to examine myself and decide in any situation if I really needed more power, and if I did, how having it would serve myself and others in a more positive and productive way. Sometimes, as in the street gang situation with the armed boy, I didn't need to have more power, and I saw how giving it up was actually more powerful than humiliating him in front of his friends, which might have gotten me or someone else killed.

As you can see, power at home and in the outside world can be both constructive and destructive. At its worst, it can destroy friendships, and families, and you can lose your job by abusing it; entire countries have also been destroyed by it, and people's quest for it. In order for us to have power of any quality over other people, we must also have leadership qualities and stewardship. This means an ability to compassionately and thoughtfully enforce rules or values, whether it be as a parent, in a job as a boss to someone else, as a mate, or as a friend.

Why is this important?

We grow up seeing power as a kind of status symbol we must attain, either because of low self-worth, or because we instinctively feel that all of us are essentially the same, so when someone has more than we do, we question why. As we get older, power becomes more about influence and control we can exert in our own lives and on those around us. True power, however, is a lot different.

What does power mean for you?

- If you're a parent, think about how your kids are responding to you. Are they respectful? Are they good listeners, and do they contribute to the welfare of the family (helping around the house, doing chores without pay) if they are old enough? Kids have a natural way of exercising their power over their parents: wearing their parents out with complaints or negative behavior, and making them feel guilty when the kids don't get what they want. You have only two ways to respond. The first is to exercise your authority with punishment, and the second is to teach them the correct way to function in a family. The first is not the Shaolin method, because in the temples the older monks teach the younger ones how to live, work, and do kung fu properly by teaching them, not through punishment.

- If you're a teenager and you want more freedom and respect from your parents, you could torture them, and make their life miserable, by rebelling. This is not what the Shaolin monks would do, but it is a sure way to self-destruction and pain. You won't win any fans if you take this approach, and you'll hurt yourself and your parents in the process. More important, you won't have any power. You'll just be obnoxious. The correct way to gain real power is to contribute to the welfare of the family, and demonstrate that you are very responsible by abiding by your parents' rules, treating your parents and siblings with respect, and doing well in school. Then you will have more freedom and power to do what you want, because you will have earned it for yourself, and in the eyes of others.

> If you are a person who is having problems at work as a boss, and can't get your staff to perform the way you would like, you *could* threaten them with taking their jobs away, or giving them tasks that they hate. Or you could treat them disrespectfully. The monks would not approve. They would say that you treat people with respect to gain respect, and that this is true power. You could let your staff know that you *respect* their ability to do their job, and that since they are experts in their field, you are there to assist them and to do whatever you can to enhance their performance and improve the quality of their lives. This approach will probably get you the results you want, you'll still have your title, and your staff will turn in better results. People want to be recognized for their talents, regardless of what the job is: this means that everyone from the person who waxes the floor in your office building to the person attempting to find the next cure for cancer is looking for respect and kindness. This means recognizing that we all want essentially the same things in life and that no one is that much different from us, and then treating others accordingly.

FINDING YOUR TRUE POWER

To get anywhere near real power, it's important to understand how easily power can be misunderstood. To demonstrate this in my classes, I perform a simple exercise. I ask the biggest, strongest-looking kid to come to the front of the mats. "Spread your legs a little wider than your shoulders" I say, "and bend your knees into a half squat." This is called the "horse stance," and it is the foundation of Shaolin kung fu (see appendix A) and most other martial arts because it makes you very strong and solid. Then I warn the student that I'll be pushing him with all my force from the side, attempting to shove him out of his stance and onto the mat. I can't tell you how often the person smirks—not having a very good grasp of physics—thinking about how difficult that will probably be. And so I proceed, using both of my hands and my own body weight, to try to push the student over. At this point, the student with the smirk is right: I often cannot move him, as it is virtually impossible to do so from where I'm standing.

I continue to push. I'm practically groaning with the effort, and the student's expression of confidence keeps building. "Give up, man," he sometimes says. I press on. When I think he is about as overconfident as he's going to get—and the people watching also feel that I won't be able to move the student—I take one finger and give a slight push on the person's chest. *Ninety-nine percent of the time*, he falls right over onto his back, and the push has taken little or no effort on my part. The result? The person who felt like King Kong for a while now feels powerless and without control. The onlookers are always as stunned as the student.

The lesson? Together, the student and I have demonstrated that although the Shaolin horse stance is extremely powerful in one direction, it's very weak in another. This is the yin-yang principle of opposites and balance again: as the great Chinese warrior Sun Tzu wrote twenty-five hundred years ago, "In strength, there is weakness, and in weakness there is strength."

True power starts with accepting that you cannot control many of the things that happen to you, no matter how strong you are. For example, your children will grow up, get married, and leave you to start a new life of their own. To many parents, this is a major loss, and they will work very hard to keep their children close, even when they are adults. Or friends and family will get sick, and some of them will die prematurely. You may lose many of the things you have spent your whole life accumulating, like wealth. Many of the things that you think will never happen to *you*, will, and no matter how powerful you perceive yourself to be, you will not have the power to stop them. You could be "the most powerful" CEO on the planet—controlling the lives of millions with a single phone call. But if that's your definition of power, how powerful will you feel when you're old and dying, and don't control any of the companies and employees you once had?

As we know by now, this is a primary Buddhist belief. To know true power is to accept that many things you work so hard to prevent will happen anyway, and that when that time comes, you must find the true power to deal with it. True power—which can also be looked at as success in any endeavor—starts with accepting that there are some things in life we simply cannot change or control (like a bad childhood or a debilitating illness), and that the only real rules of life are the ones we create for ourselves, and the ones life itself dictates. These rules of society—that you have to go to college to be a success, or you need to make a million dollars to be considered truly powerful—are completely arbitrary.

WHAT ARE THE "RULES" OF SUCCESS, TO WESTERNERS?

What does success mean to us? Better yet, what have we been programmed to believe success is?

- You are a loser without a college education.

- There must be "something wrong with you" if you are a woman and not married by the age of thirty—and worse, if you haven't produced any grandchildren.

- You dropped out of law school, so you're a failure. Or you graduated from law school but became a nurse instead because you wanted to help people in a very different way. People think you're weird for doing so.

- You are seven feet tall and hate basketball; or you're five foot three and love to play basketball, but everyone laughs even though you're good at it.

- If you were a woman with children in the 1950s and had a career, you were frowned upon, and considered a bad parent.

> If you were a woman with children in the 1990s and had a career, you were not frowned upon; in fact, you were considered a pioneer.

These are just a few examples of how society's "rules" are plainly ridiculous. Only you can define the rules for your own success. Only you can find power in knowing that you are doing the right thing, and when you live your life this way, everyone benefits. There are millions of examples of people who break these rules and redefine them for themselves every day.

Life gives you what you give to it, and everyone around you is deserving of what you have to offer, and your kindness.

After many years of getting kicked around by life and being angry about it, I now know very well that the force behind my punches or kicks can kill, just as readily as the inner-city kids I work with know that pulling the trigger will take someone's life. But neither of these responses makes me, or them, truly powerful. I've learned that real power is the power to truly know what you want, for yourself and your life, so that you don't make rash decisions based on anger, but powerful ones based on thought and observation. Nothing's harder, because it means letting go of old thought patterns where you think power is jumping into a fight or making a million more than the next guy. But it's not.

Napoleon once said, "The most dangerous moment in battle is victory." I never forgot this quote. Victory is dangerous because the more we win, the more powerful we think we are, and the more careless we may become in our dealings with others. Thinking we are more powerful leads to abusing our power and believing ourselves invincible. This is when we get careless, make mistakes; and so we can eventually be taken down by our enemies (and sometimes . . . we *are* the enemy), which has happened consistently throughout history, and will continue to happen unless we as a society begin to make some serious changes.

True power goes far beyond our individual dreams and desires. It's bigger than that—and it's bigger than we are. It means recognizing that we are essentially powerless, drifting around on this planet in the cosmos, but we are also all connected to this same fate, whether we like to admit it or not. We all go through the same issues—anger, fear, insecurity, self-worth,—so if people are happy in this country and miserable everywhere else in the world, how long do you think we're going to stay happy?

Therefore, the key to true power is understanding who we are and what we want, and then achieving our individual goals of personal happiness, power, or success so that we can one day help others to achieve their goals as well. Once we do that, we will not only be unlocking the true power within ourselves, but helping the world function in a much more loving, compassionate, and natural way.

10

YOU CAN'T MOVE ON IF YOU CAN'T LET GO

When we look at a statue of someone great, we
think they've got something we don't. We are
trained to think that only a very tiny percentage
of us will ever have what it takes to be a hero.
Not many of us will win the Nobel Prize, cure
any diseases or slay any dragons, but every
single one of us is called to be a king or a queen,
a hero in our own ordinary lives. Statues are not
built to honor the exceptional life, they are built
to remind us what is possible in our own.

—AUTHOR UNKNOWN

LOVING YOURSELF AND LETTING IT ALL GO

My brother Billy never found happiness. He thought he
would be happy, and his life would be validated, if he could
get closure on his past and be accepted by a specific group of
people. He died trying.

Billy was my half brother by my mom, and because we had
different dads, I thought we were very different. He and I
never got along because he was the golden child to my stepdad, Mitch, and I could do no right by Mitch, not being his bi-

ological son like Billy. This didn't change much as we got older.

Billy had a multitude of problems, in spite of being "most favored son," a title I did everything I could to earn from Mitch. One of the worst of Billy's disabilities was his severe dyslexia. At the time, the school systems did not have the sophistication they do now in assessing and treating dyslexia, and thus Billy was labeled "learning disabled" and put in a class with very slow learners. Billy was in fact very smart, and when he was tested years later, his IQ was off the charts.

Billy never accomplished much in his life. He went from job to job, state to state, always borrowing money from my sisters and me, and often returning home penniless. Eventually Billy moved to San Francisco, and there he stayed. I don't remember when I figured out that he might be gay, because it was never discussed or accepted in the family, just suspected. To say we were not close would be an understatement; as a result, I never knew what he did for a living, but was aware that his need to borrow money never ceased. Every so often, when he hadn't called for yet another loan in a while, I'd find out how Billy was from my mom.

During one of our many conversations, she told me that Billy had AIDS. I really didn't react, because Billy always— and I mean always—lied. He had been a fibber since he was a kid, maybe in an effort to make his reality better than it was. He lied about his girlfriends, his grades, where he was working, the money he made, and the people he knew, so I didn't believe this latest piece of information, either—and not for the right reason, which was that it would make a terrible truth.

Sadly, this particular bit of news turned out to be true. Billy did have AIDS, and he was slowly dying. It took a while, but as happens with AIDS, Billy just disintegrated, and another call a couple of years later came from my sister Michelle telling me that he wasn't expected to live much longer. She asked me go to San Francisco with her to see him because he had told her that he didn't want to come home to die in my mother's house. I grudgingly said I would go.

When I got there I was shocked to see what he looked like. Billy was always a big boy like his dad—consistently over two hundred pounds. Now he weighed less than a hundred. It killed me to see him this way because although I never liked him, I wanted to love him as my brother. Billy asked if I would talk to him without anyone else around, and it turned out to be the saddest conversation of my life.

He wanted to make peace with me. He said he was sorry for everything he had put my mom and me through. His life as a gay man, he said, had been very promiscuous sexually, and now he was paying for it. Billy said that he didn't regret the fact that he was gay, because the people he had met and befriended as a gay-identified man had been good to him, but he regretted being so promiscuous. "But, Stevie," he said softly, "the men always liked me, and they accepted me for who I was."

All Billy wanted in life was to be accepted, and to have some validation for who he truly was; at the end of it all, dying of a terrible disease, this was the only thing that mattered to him. He didn't care whether he'd done anything good for the world, or for his family, or for his lover. He just wanted people to believe in him. As pathetic as it was, I could see myself in his yearnings, and how I had long had the same desire for acceptance in my own way. Billy and I were not so different after all.

In fact, we weren't so different from many other people who climb uphill by seeking some kind of belief and acceptance, whether it is from other people or themselves. The original monks, too, were not exempt from this kind of human desire: they wanted to learn the true meaning of life to validate their own existence, so they could have something higher to believe in. They wanted to be accepted as monks by the great masters, and thought that if they could learn and understand the true way, they could have some control over lessening the suffering of humanity. That's about as selfless a goal as a human can have, but it was still all in the service of the monks' own need for acceptance.

THE MOUNTAIN AND THE WAY

A Zen master living as a hermit on a mountain was asked by a monk, "What is the way?"

"What a fine mountain this is," the master replied.

"I am not asking about the mountain. I am asking about the way."

The master replied, "So long as you cannot go beyond the mountain, my son, you cannot reach the way."

A few years ago, I finally figured out what the Zen master was trying to say. My entire existence in life had been made up of climbing mountains, each one different in complexity and in size. Each time I encountered a mountain in the past, whether it was a personal challenge or a professional one, I would always "conquer" the mountain; some were more difficult to get past than others. Every time I got to the top of my Mount Everest, I felt good, I felt validated, and I would look around for acceptance from other great mountain climbers.

This time, I thought, *surely* someone will notice and believe in me—make me part of their family, or club, or friendship circle. Because I was approaching the mountains for the wrong reasons—I never felt that I had done enough, or tried hard enough—before long I was looking for another mountain to climb, never being happy with summiting the previous one.

It took me a long time to realize that maybe *I* was the mountain, and unless I was able to understand who and what I was really trying to reach, I would be climbing mountains forever, until one day I would die, still trying, like my brother Billy—without ever knowing the way.

Monks see the "mountain" not as something to get past to move forward on your journey, but as an obstacle to evaluate, understand, and raze by realizing that you probably created it, and you can get past it only by identifying what sort of emotional or spiritual roadblock it represents for you.

I remember that I would get aggravated with Shaolin Buddhist philosophy when it made me look at who I was being in the world, rather than how I appeared to others in it. We have the ability to make others think we are someone we are not; so we often appear to others in dress or some other way that we would like to see ourselves: in an expensive car, at a high-end party, giving money to a charity so our names will be on its board—and the list goes on.

In my Shaolin training, I had to learn the hard reality of actually seeing who I was and accepting the man looking back at me in the mirror. I knew that I could *appear* to be who I wanted to be—complete with expensive cars, nice clothes, and so on—and I could also act out who I wanted to be, but inevitably, at home alone, I would always see myself as I actually was.

Sometimes I liked what I saw, and sometimes I hated it. With focused physical and mental training, the "true you"—maybe the one you've been hiding from for years—will always appear, though at first, many times, it will slide right by you because you don't want to look at it. I knew I had character flaws, and I knew that I would be forced to really look at them through my training with the great masters: I could never fool them, or really, myself.

This extended to my kung fu practice. When I wanted to seem knowledgeable about a form, even if I wasn't, I would ask the master if it was good enough. Inevitably, he would answer my question with what I perceived to be a totally unrelated question or statement. It made me nuts. "Work on that more," he would simply say. It didn't matter whether something *looked* right, it had to be done right, for the right reason so that *my inner being was strong*.

Of course, as a lifetime striver for answers and acceptance, I thought this was bullshit. Why the hell didn't they just give me the answers to the questions I was asking? I was trying to learn, and they weren't helping. How could I be expected to get better? Then, some years ago, I reread that old Shaolin passage about the mountain and "the way," and I learned something new.

The monk who was asking the question—and not getting the answer he wanted—had become a monk because he believed that there could be a better life, a life that had meaning and would explain his place in the cosmos, otherwise known as "validation." Before that conversation, I figured monks were a higher type of species, in a sense; they didn't "need" the things a man like me needed because their lives were so ascetic. They didn't "need" validation for their abilities, I thought, just as they didn't *need* sex, or love, or money. As it turns out, wanting validation or acceptance is a human quality; all men who desire to be monks join the temple to learn and seek enlightenment so they can be validated for their existence, just as I did.

But I didn't get what I was looking for, because my teaching Shaolin to other people wasn't supposed to be about me getting thanks, it was about believing that working to help other people was its own reward. I just didn't get this at the time. When I first began to work with troubled people, I expected that my efforts toward kindness would be acknowledged, because I was still repeating my patterns from childhood. I thought that for every kindness I did, my students would come back to me, put their arms around me, and say, "I love you, Steve. Thanks." More often than not, that did not happen. I was constantly disappointed by the people around me, and saddened by what I perceived to be their lack of appreciation. It wasn't until I looked into the roots of why I felt I needed my efforts to be validated that I began to see the truth.

For us to really understand why we have the need to be accepted and validated, we have to look at where we came from and how we were raised. You've heard this before, but it's true. There are two driving forces that help shape the kind of person we become. Usually, a boy will try to pattern his life after things his dad does, and a girl will look to her mother for guidance in the same way. If your dad or mom was an overachiever, then you will most likely measure yourself by how you live up to his or her standards.

In my case, my mom was a superwoman and my dad was a loser. I lived with my mom; therefore she had greater influence over my behavior and beginnings than a mother generally would with a boy child. Even though my mom was a superwoman, however, she spent her own life working to be good enough, I believe, so she could feel accepted and validated in spite of her disabilities. Had she really believed in herself and what she had accomplished—disabled or not— she would not have gotten remarried, after she left my father, to another abusive man.

I realized I was just like my mom in my need for acceptance: I always wanted everyone to love me, and I figured this would validate my existence. What took me so long to accept was that no matter how hard I tried, it would be impossible to please all people, all the time. How many times have you said to yourself, "I don't care what anyone thinks about me?" Is that really the truth? In actuality, most people may say that because they're proud or don't want to seem self-involved, but the truth of the matter is, many of us are thinking, I *wish* I didn't care what others thought about me.

True self-acceptance comes when we stop worrying about "being somebody" and start focusing on being okay with who we are; if we're not okay with who we are, then every day, again, there are chances to change our behavior, and *that's* where our focus should be.

I used to say that my life was always about wanting to "be somebody." I now realize I was *always* "somebody." I just didn't know it. I was too stuck in the past, only seeing what I didn't have, always moving on to the next project and never acknowledging that I'd finished the first, and never sitting down and saying, "Hey, Stevie, if you don't think you're somebody, why is that?" The reason was that I kept trying to make others see my worth instead of seeing it for myself.

Confucius said, "The man who finds happiness is better than the one who loves it." One of the definitions of being happy for many people with low self-esteem (as I have grappled with throughout my life) is seeking acceptance and validation for their actions and existence, since we never got that to begin with. Once that acceptance and validation come, we feel happy. But that only lasts a short time. It's fleeting because it's not real happiness. Real happiness comes when we have a solid understanding of ourselves and our place in the world, not when we go searching for happiness as a means to fill the void in our lives that should have been filled early on, or right now, through some hard self-examination.

Many of us *know* the truth about ourselves. We know that we're pushovers in our relationships, or that we yearn for approval. However, most of us don't do anything about it. We ignore it because it's painful to acknowledge, and it's also painful to work through, because it means going back to the past, understanding how that behavior got started, and then constantly reinforcing a change in that pattern.

NO TIME LIKE THE PRESENT

In 1993 I was at a private event in Martha's Vineyard with Jan Paschal, the U.S. Department of Education's national representative, with whom I often traveled on behalf of then president Clinton. The mayor of Brockton was there, and Jan was trying to get me to return to Brockton High School to make a speech to the current student body. I flat out refused, and realized that I was still harboring far too much resentment against the school for the riot that had happened thirty-odd years before: this wasn't very Shaolin. When the mayor heard about the work I had done with inner-city kids over the years, he urged me to come and speak alongside a handful of Clinton's cabinet members and appointees to the Department of Education.

Every year the U.S. Department of Education sponsors a program in schools across the country called "America Goes Back to School," for which they profile a dozen schools and pay a great deal of public attention to the ones chosen. By the end of the event, Jan, the president, and the mayor had decided that that coming fall, Brockton High would be one of them, and I should be the keynote speaker. I couldn't turn down President Clinton. Dressed casually in slacks and a polo shirt, this high-powered guy, who by this time addressed me by first name, leveled me as he did everyone else with his charisma and conviction. "Do it for the kids, Steve, like you always do," he drawled.

Will McDonough, one of the most famous sportswriters in the country, called me to do a big article on my return to Brockton. I wondered if anyone had gotten ahold of Vinnie Vecchioni, who I thought would be an excellent complement to my story. If people could read how one person changed everything for a troubled young boy, I figured that might be the best way of explaining why I had made it, who was responsible, and how I later tried to live my life based on a philosophy of change and compassion. I directed all the reporters to call him if they *really* wanted a good story about helping kids in Brockton.

And then I found myself back in Brockton six months later, roaming the back roads around the projects in my car the night before my speech. I was restless, unsettled by the notion that for all my visible material success, I was still troubled by even a brief return, even though speaking was meant to be an honor. Hadn't I done enough to escape my past? Wasn't I "somebody" yet? Didn't all the awards I had received make me a different—and maybe a better—person? I realized that in trying to leave my past behind, in a way ignoring who I was and where I came from, I wasn't as far evolved as I had thought.

The next day, I was the last person to speak. With about a thousand hard-core kids in the audience, I had to follow deputy assistant secretary of the department of education Wilson Goode, who was generally doing a good job in the White House but that night said the most asinine thing. "From Washington," he offered, "we just want you to know that even though you kids don't respect yourselves, we respect you." When I heard Goode—who is a black man—say that to the primarily black audience, I knew we were in trouble. And sure enough, we were. The kids started yelling and booing, and one girl began to throw a violent tantrum: with the cabinet member watching, four teachers had to lift her from the audience and carry her out of the auditorium. Yelling obscenities too foul to repeat, the girl could be heard railing against Goode and his thoughtless comment long after she was removed.

It took a few minutes to quiet the student body down again, and me being a white guy taking the podium didn't help things. I started talking: mostly I talked about my experiences at Brockton High and how I'd had to raise myself up out of poverty and hardship. I told funny stories about my bodyguard, a black guy named Dennis who had protected me, how I could dance better than the black guys, and how I came back to Brockton because Bill Clinton made me. But mostly I told them about Vinnie Vecchioni, and how he had mentored me and saved my life.

The kids responded. They were laughing, silent, or crying at intervals. I think it was probably the most powerful talk I've ever given. Better, it was a great personal relief that I didn't bomb, because even though I had given hundreds of speeches over the years, this one seemed one of the hardest to deliver.

The mayor took the stage and thanked me for my talk. Then he announced that he had a surprise for me. Out walked Vinnie, whom I hadn't seen for twenty years. We embraced, and I was unable to speak, though I wanted desperately to thank him for everything he'd done for me, and to tell him that I loved him. The kids looking on were silent, and when Vinnie and I finally let go of each other, I saw that many of them—hardened gang members, unwed mothers, and drug dealers—were crying too. It was one of the best days of my life. I had come home, I felt loved, and I realized I was exactly where I was supposed to be—even in Brockton.

The Shaolin masters would say of the time it took me to realize all this, "That didn't take very long at all!" That's the way they think. It's the path you've journeyed on, and the experience itself, that finally lead to a sort of personal enlightenment. To the monks, enlightenment is getting so close to Buddhahood that you become like a Buddha. But they recognize, as I do now, that they may never reach that final level of experience, because there are just some things we can't control. But as long as they spend every day in the moment of working toward their goal, helping themselves, helping others, being more compassionate, and accepting where they are on any given day, that is good enough.

What is your goal? What do you want out of life?

Remember, life is short, so there's no better time to start living it than now.

GAINING CLOSURE ON ABUSE

My mother, Carol, had a hard time telling me why people did bad things. She was especially tight-lipped about my dad, Al, and why he touched me. A child doesn't understand sexual abuse, and it is impossible to explain in its perversity. My father told me we did those things because if a son loves his dad, that's what you do. And I loved him to death, so that's what I did.

He had visiting rights after my parents split up, and every Saturday morning my dad would pick me up and take me to his place. Al had an apartment on New York's Upper East Side, not far from where we lived. We'd walk there or take a cab when he had money, which was almost never. My legs were short, and the walk was long, but never long enough to get away from the small dark room where he lived.

My sister Michelle told me that my mother knew my father was abusing me. My mother, because she was disabled and had grown up in the care of a Catholic hospital run by nuns, was afraid of losing me. She worried that the state would come and take me away. As she saw it, she had an eighth-grade education, and had four fingers on one hand and wooden legs—so what sort of mother would social services think she could be? Al, a manipulative asshole, told her that if she shared what he did to me with anyone, he would go to the state and tell them that Mom wasn't capable of taking care of me. And so she was fearful, and sad, and silent.

I used to watch Al beat my mom too; I remember him smacking her, and knocking her down on the couch. I was so angry when I'd see my mom crying, and felt completely helpless. I wanted to kill my father for his abuse of my mother and me, but I loved him. It was this weird, unconditional love that kept me locked in a pattern of hating and worshipping him for many years, and, even after he disappeared, from getting closure on my relationship with him. But something had to give: I was miserable, and I needed to find a way to shut the memories out, and put them to rest.

A large part of using Shaolin in your life involves getting closure on events and situations that have not worked out for you. A lot of this has to do with letting go of old habits and ideas, which we all know die hard. In these times we need to remember that everything connects, and that people do bad things because that's what they were taught. They are repeating a pattern that was probably handed down by their parents, and the only way to break that cycle is by making the decision to do it now.

Many people recognize their problems, but don't rectify them because of fear: a fear of making mistakes, perhaps, or of losing something, or the sense that they'll be punished for an action. As soon as one starts to look at letting go, fear comes into the equation. Overcoming fear is not easy, but what can help is remembering that fear will never go away unless it's faced. Even if you lock it away in the darkest part of your soul, it will find a way out—in your relationships, in your personal issues, everywhere. It will seep into your life in ways you never even expected, until it is finally confronted and let go.

The details of how I was abused will always be horrifying. That part will never change, and my shame and confusion as a child increased every time I visited my dad's dim little shit hole of an apartment. Many of us have a dark room of some kind in our past, and the pain of it never fully disappears, no matter what we do. It doesn't matter what lived in *your* dark room—an abusive relationship, failing at something, lost love, an unethical decision you made—it can be hard to face, and then get over. Closure—particularly surrounding an abusive situation—is definitely one of the toughest steps to address on your path, because when we look at the crises of our lives, we're often dealing with ghosts, or at least very old, deep-rooted memories that have acted as the blueprints for our entire lives. It took me a very long time to figure out how to get past those images I had of my dad every time I closed my eyes, day or night. But I did. And you can too.

THE ASSHOLE THEORY

I mentioned this earlier, but it deserves repeating and highlighting. Nobody wants to be an asshole. And believe it or not, the concept, though I've Americanized it, is also Shaolin.

What "Nobody wants to be as asshole" means is that all people are basically good. So if they are angry or mean or abusive, it's because bad and unpleasant things have happened to them. They might not change these things anytime soon, and they might always be assholes no matter what we say or do. But if we can at least acknowledge that they had this history—which was probably very painful as well—it can help us get closure for ourselves.

Children don't understand parental abuse, whether it is sexual, physical, or emotional. Most young people believe their abusive parent or parents love them, but are very confused about this twisted relationship between anger and affection. "How can these terrible things happen, and how could our parents make these mistakes?" I have often been asked. My dad beat my mother and sexually abused me repeatedly for years. Why? Because of the abuse and pain *he* went through in his life. Now I realize that my father loved me in spite of what he did, and was not capable of carrying on a normal life.

Realizing that parents are human, that they make mistakes, and that their inadequacy as parents really isn't their fault, helps children diffuse some of their anger. Most important, the children come to understand that a parent's questionable behavior is not his or her fault, regardless of the fact that abuse—in any form—is never okay, and should never be tolerated by anyone.

THE FINE LINE BETWEEN HATE AND FORGIVENESS

My father was a deranged young man, and he eventually became a pathetic, deranged old man. The last time I saw him, it was with the intention of killing him, as he had driven my grandmother to attempt suicide.

I went to see Al for the first time in years at a shitty boardinghouse he was living in. I was sixteen, and had not been exposed to Shaolin yet. Coming down the stairs, Al was nothing like I remembered him. He was smaller, thinner, and more stooped. Age and his sickness had withered him.

I felt the hard outline of the knife handle in my pocket, and there was no doubt in my mind that I was going to kill him. He was already dead to me, this man who hurt everyone and everything—including me—and now my grandmother. "Let's go to my room and talk," he said. The tiny room could not have been more than four by eight feet, with a narrow cot and a beat-up bureau wedged in by the window.

Immediately on entering the room, I went from rage to pity. Just like that, I loved my father again and wanted to take care of him. Though I thought I had forgiven him for abusing me as a child, all those memories came rushing back. "Dad, I can't talk in here," I said. "Can we go for coffee somewhere?" At a nearby diner, we did talk. We talked about his life, and his treatment of our family. "I haven't had a great life, Stevie," he said, stirring black coffee and not meeting my eyes. "I regret a lot of things. I don't have any excuses."

And that was it. We finished our coffee, and he paid for it. There wasn't much left to say, and during our slow walk back to the rooming house I kept my hands in my pockets and fingered the knife, thinking about what I had come there to do, and how much my thinking could change in an hour. That day, I chose to see a life in all of its sadness and complexity instead of taking one.

There was no real good-bye between us. "See you," said Al, his eyes cast down at the ground. "Yeah, see you, Dad," I said, and watched him disappear into the shadow of the building. I never saw my father again after that.

Then, I almost made a classic mistake: continuing to allow

abusive behavior to seep over from our childhood into our adult lives.

When I got home from that last visit with my dad, I felt sad but calm and collected. Or so I thought. Not only did I no longer want to kill him, I told my mom that I was going to move back to New York so that I could take care of him. My mom, who worried about having only an eighth-grade education, had a lot of wisdom, and hearing this, she nearly killed me herself. Here was Carol, a woman who made a practice of not hitting me as a child, ready to kill me to save me. I could probably count on the fingers of one hand the times she raised her voice to me, but that day pushed it to another five fingers.

Then Carol got quiet. I'll never forget what she said. "Go and live with him if you want," she sneered. "He will ruin your life like he ruined ours." I learned that day that she had left my dad and taken me with her to spare our lives. Even as I look back years later, I realize I knew then that there was a major distinction between understanding your abuser's problems and allowing yourself to be abused any longer. Dad would have kept abusing me in whatever way I allowed him to. That's who he was, and he certainly wasn't going to change, so my pain and suffering would have continued.

Later, when I gained more knowledge about human behavior, I applied the asshole theory to my relationship with my dad. Instead of looking at what he had done to me, I started looking at what was done to him, and began to ask questions. What could make a man like him have a son like me, who at sixteen had survived everything he did to me, and poverty to boot? How could a demented guy like this get my mother, a woman who was loving and smart, to marry him? I examined his life to learn as much as I could about where he came from: I went back, talked to my mother, and found out what

Al's father had done to him, and how abused *he* had been.

Perspective is an amazing gift. My dad's dad used to kick him across the room and beat him unmercifully. I thought about what that must have been like for him. Then, right after he beat Al half to death, my grandfather would go in and hug him and tell him how much he loved him. With a sense of this ass-backward way of administering "love" and "care," I gained an understanding of what Al had been through, and this helped me to think about my pain *differently*. Don't get me wrong, the pain was still there. Perspective didn't lessen what I was going through, but it did help me understand what was happening so that I could better help myself. Instead of getting angry at everyone because they destroyed my life, I was able to see that I was just another link on a chain, and if I didn't stop the cycle of abuse, it would continue. This knowledge helped turn my negative thoughts and behaviors into positive change.

When I decide to spend a day at a shelter for battered women, talking to abused women about protecting themselves, dealing with how badly they have been hurt, and how they can consider changing their lives for the better, I think of my mom, and my father beating her. I couldn't help her or myself at that time, but *I can try to help these women now*. If I see kids in the streets that need guidance because they have been raised poor, and without a good education or with abusive or negligent parents, I try to use the pain I experienced in my own childhood to help them, because in them I see myself.

Once I learned to apply the Asshole Theory to my dad's way of treating me, I was able to get some perspective on the memory of abuse, acknowledge and mourn it so it did not build up, and then ultimately let it go. The issues I encountered because of those times—like not believing in myself, low self-esteem, anger, rage, loss—have made my life very difficult, but they did not destroy it. What he did to me will never truly "go away," but by deciding to change my approach to feeling the pain, I am able to move forward and live.

THE DYNAMIC CYCLE OF LIFE AND DEATH

Death is probably one of the toughest life experiences to get closure on. My mother's death could have killed me; she was my hero, and my support system. Although I was grieving beyond belief for this woman who was most important in my life, I fought inertia.

A discussion of death and closure in Western terms is difficult to do within the context of Buddhism, because the Shaolin, like all Buddhists, believe in reincarnation. This means living the most compassionate life you can because that governs what or who you come back as. Whether you believe in this or not, we're all like the monks in the sense that when someone we love dies, it affects us because we "desire" to see them alive again, somehow, somewhere.

All Buddhists believe suffering is caused by desire, and in the case of death, if you want to end your sense of suffering, then you must let go of your desire to see someone else live. Obviously, at the time of a loved one's death, this seems emotionally impossible because we are so used to her being around. We are attached to her, as we're attached to an arm or a leg, and if one of those things should be cut off, you'd feel pain no matter what!

But the Buddhists have a point. . . .

We would be much better able to accept death as a natural thing if we didn't dress it up in this culture by putting a negative connotation on it. While children are taught about life and birth through storybooks about babies and little animals, you'll find far fewer books about death. But death is a natural dynamic of life, just like being born. We get sad because of our attachment not only to that person, but to what he or she represented for us and in our lives. When a close relative dies, that shifts the perspective around, and you have to try and find meaning in it. We fight this by thinking death is senseless, but that's just crazy because it's a reality none of us can change. We're all going to die. The pain of attachment is there no matter what, but we can help ourselves move through this pain by remembering that life goes on.

When a loved one dies, most people feel as if they are dying too. They cry, hit furniture, ignore the kids, walk around dejected for days, and the list goes on and on. But who is this about? The person who died doesn't need you to mourn like that to know you loved and cared for him. In fact, if he saw you wrecking your own life, he'd probably come back and swat you in the head. We need to take the focus off of ourselves—how this death is affecting us—and start putting it back to where it needs to be—on the people we loved.

I went to my mother's funeral without any of this analysis, of course, and there were so many people there: nearly three hundred cars brought mourners to say good-bye to her. I remember sitting there on a little metal chair, looking around, and having no idea who the hell they all were.

The truth was, my mother affected so many lives that they all showed up, and until that moment I'd had no idea she was so well known for her many contributions to the lives of other people—which only made my grief that much worse. Carol had tons of gubernatorial and senatorial awards for her work with disadvantaged, poor parents, those who wanted a better life for themselves and their children. I just sat there and wondered what had happened, and why, as we do when we lose someone we love.

Still, the first thing I did after my mother died—in spite of my intense feelings of loss and anger over the fact that she was gone—was to go back to my kung fu studio. Two days later, I was back training people again. No one could understand how I could do such a thing. Didn't I have to grieve? they asked. The most important person to me was gone, and did I really want to be watching kids do kicks and punches? No, I wanted to sit down and cry, but I also understood that death could take over my life—destroying everything good I had built up over many years—my family, my business, and my relationships.

Somehow, I understood that there was *nothing* that I could do to change the reality of my mother's death. Strangely, I didn't have this attitude because she would have wanted me to soldier on or anything else as honorable. In fact, a lot of behavioral scientists would call my going right back to work "denial," but in actuality it was probably the most positive distraction to help me deal with my pain. They'd say that when you go to the grave and stand over the casket, you're "dealing" with the death, but I think that's part of what keeps you stuck in grief, and backing away from closure.

Death is a strange thing: even as it takes our loved ones away, it has the potential to kill us in the aftermath if we let it. I have many times seen in elderly couples that when one of the spouses passes away, the other one will die shortly after. The point is, if you let the death of a relative or friend—or even something simpler like the loss of a job—paralyze you, you'll end up ignoring other priorities you may have; like children, or your partner, or even the dog that relies on you to feed and care for it. By holding on to something that is already gone, we begin to step out of the natural dynamic of life and create a kind of alternate, limbo reality for ourselves, where we don't move, we get nothing done, and we stop living, as if we were the ones that died.

ANYONE CAN CHANGE THE WORLD

When a man decides to become a Shaolin monk, the past is left behind and he begins life all over again. He learns to retrain and rebuild his body and mind so that he might prepare for the overwhelming sacrifice and duty of serving this world. This requires an incredible amount of belief—in what he's doing, in who he is, in why he's doing it, and that the outcome will be okay, no matter what.

Sometimes it might seem that Shaolin monks don't have it as bad as we do. They don't have to deal with the day-to-day grind of a job they hate, a partner yelling at them because they came home late without calling, or the hundreds of other distractions we find in our own world. But clearing the mind and rebuilding ourselves from the bottom up is the same whether you're doing it in a small village or a massive city. It takes hard work, focus, discipline, and a strong will to understand ourselves and the world we live in.

Believing in yourself means having a clear definition of who you are. It means remembering the things about yourself that can help you—stepping-stones to get you where you need to be. If you are kind and sensitive, if you can shoot a mean game of pool, if you listen well or have overcome adversity in the past, all of these things can remind you of who you are. Once you figure that out, you have a foundation on which to build. Like Shaolin monks who first don a robe and begin their training anew, it is only with a clear sense of who we are that we can know what we want, where we want to go, and why.

Throughout your journey in life, you have been climbing mountains, as I did for many years. Maybe you had to deal with low self-worth, parents that were never around, unspeakable tragedies, or simply moving through life with no direction, purpose, or understanding of what it all means. By now however, I hope you can see that if you look over your shoulder, back down the road you've just traveled, the reality is that you have *always* had power over your life. You didn't get to decide who your parents were, where you were born, or how you were initially raised, but then again, you can't control everything, can you?

What you can control is what you do from this day forward. You can accept that you're unhappy with certain situations in your life, and you can change them. In truth, the only real mountains we have ever had to climb are the ones we have created for ourselves—by staying in anger over things we can't control, by not getting the help we need because of fear, by expecting that the world owes us something for what we've had to go through, etc., etc., etc. Those are just excuses. You are not a victim. No one is. You are a warrior, and you have always been, which is why you're still here, and why you're reading this book.

Mark Twain once said something to the effect of, "Every day, a child is born that could change the world. Unfortunately, we don't know which child that is, so we must take care of each and every one of them." In the end, if we do not help ourselves, we cannot help anyone else, and if we can't do that, what's the point?

We are all one, whether we like it or not. Sure, at the beginning of our journey it may seem that someone who's prettier or wealthier or more confident than we are is somehow better off than we are, but in reality that's not true. He or she might have more money and confidence, but we all have to go through the same things. We all deal with anger, loss, regret, and our place in the world. The only thing that's different is the cards we were dealt. We all live on the same planet. We all feel that pit of loneliness in our stomachs that we try so hard to fill with everything from food to drugs to work. But that void can never be filled with external objects. It can be filled only by recognizing the truth—that we are not alone. When we help others, we are reminded of this fact. When we help ourselves, we grow even stronger.

I have always liked the quote I started this chapter with, and use it often to close my speeches, because it suggests a message of acceptance of both our right place in the world and where we are in it now. No matter who you are, or what level of success or notoriety you reach in life, you are still a wheel in the machine, and you can make a difference.

Be your own king, your own queen, your own hero, if you must. Stare up at statues, and live into the possibility of becoming the kindest and most fulfilled person you can be as you go through your days. But while you're looking up, or ahead, or behind—at real people or statues made to show honor and remind of possibility—remember to look in the mirror. Who do you see? What do you stand for? And when you go down the road, finding your way, always remember that if we are all connected, you are not six steps removed from being a Shaolin warrior . . . you *are* one.

AFTERWORD

Throughout my life and its hardships, I've come to believe that destiny is a balance between fate and action. You can't control the cards you're dealt, but you certainly don't have to sit around the table and moan and whine, either. You have to get up and make the best out of what you have, or you might as well not even play.

Many times throughout my life I have tried to figure out why I failed many times, and succeeded many times. And I've come up with what seems like a thousand different answers. Sometimes I think it's because I was born poor and abused in the ghetto and had a survivor's mentality—the harder you beat me down, the harder I would work to stand back up. It's just that I was usually the one beating myself down and then standing up again. . . .

For me, standing up eventually meant that I took the Shaolin path I've been talking about for the last thirty years: and practice what I preach. All we own in life is who we *are,* what we say we are, and how we choose to act. Everything else, no matter how much or how little we may have, can be taken away. At the end of it all, when you're lying on your deathbed, you might *have* a lot of money from all the work you did in life, but all you *own* is who you are.

But still . . . no matter how far I've come from where I began, I still have bad days. It's just that now, even in my darkest hours, I have a Shaolin mind-set that can give me hope, because it shows me by example each day that everything continues to grow and change—and nothing ever really ends. Every decision we make and every action we take has meaning, and affects everything else—now and always.

Not too long ago, something reminded me of this fact.

One of my sisters, Franny, barely ever spoke to me growing up. After our mother died, she stopped talking to me entirely. Still, one day I was driving home and got to thinking about her and how she was always the baby of the family, how I had tried to protect her from the pain of a bad dad, and the pain of poverty and all that goes along with it. I decided to pick up my cell phone and call her.

She answered the phone, and all I said was, "Franny."

"Stevie," she said softly.

I told her I loved her, and she said the same: we both cried and said we would stay in touch, and we did. Shortly after that, her son graduated from high school and Franny threw a big graduation party. She called to invite me, which would never have happened if I hadn't made that initial call.

At the party I saw a woman whom I hadn't seen since my

mother was alive. She used to work for my mother at Head Start, and was now one of the directors. She said she was looking for a keynote speaker for the upcoming year's Head Start programs, who would address all of the Head Start teachers and paraprofessionals in Brockton, Massachusetts, where I grew up. Would I be interested? she wondered. I said I would speak, no charge, in honor of my mom's work for the organization.

Now, I have given hundreds of speeches and lectures, from Harvard and Yale to the Delta in Arkansas. This was one of the hardest: speaking of my mother's life now that she was gone was tough. In that talk, I referenced an old friend of mine called Henry H., probably because I was in Brockton and it made me think of him.

I talked about how Henry beat me up when we were kids— he was a bully, and I was small. I was a student at Brockton High School at the time, and I had gone to a weekend party, had a few Colt 45s, and—bad idea—talked to Henry H.'s girl. Henry gave me the beating of my life. The next day, to my great surprise, Henry tracked me down and instead of giving me another beating, he *apologized*. This was very unusual: street kids don't do that, because it's seen as weak. I liked him immediately after that, and many times in the streets, he protected me.

I never knew why.

Many years and a wife and two kids later, I was driving down Main Street in Brockton. I would often detour through the projects when visiting my sisters nearby; I wanted to see if any of my boys were still around. As I was driving, I spotted three guys doing what appeared to be a drug transaction, and Henry H. was one of them. I had my newborn twins and my wife in the car, but my excitement at seeing Henry after all those years overtook any sense of reason.

Slamming on the brakes, I jumped out of the car, at which time the three of them reached in their pockets to pull their guns. I yelled out several times, "Henry, it's me! It's me!" Henry waved them off and yelled back, "Steve! Steve!" He embraced me several times; all he kept saying was, "Look at choo!" Henry and I talked for a few minutes before I took him over to meet my wife and kids. We talked about the guys we grew up with, and how many were in prison or had been shot; he told me he had just gotten out of an eight-year stretch for stabbing someone. Henry then told me something that would affect me for the rest of my life.

"You know, Steve," Henry said, "I always thought that if any one of us made it out of here, I'd be glad if it was you." That meant more to me than any award, because here was Henry, once so powerful I thought, and now, here he was, looking up to me, all the time rooting for me. This planted a seed that would eventually help me help someone else during that Head Start talk years later, but I didn't know it yet.

That was the last time I saw Henry H., and until I got back to Brockton, I hadn't thought of him much.

After my talk for Head Start a pretty girl about seventeen years old came up to me, and before she could get the words out, she burst into tears. When she could speak, she said, "I'm Henry's daughter. He just died last week from cancer."

I hugged her for a minute and then we sat down.

"I loved my dad, and you knew a lot about him," she said. "I knew who you were as soon as you started talking about him, because my dad always talked about you and said I should be like you." She paused. "It was really nice to hear something good about my dad." She was telling me that while Henry H. hadn't lived a very accomplished life by most people's standards, the fact that someone like me had made it out of the projects and held her dad in such high esteem meant a lot.

Looking back, I realized that a seed had been planted during my time in the projects with Henry, who bullied and then protected me, later thinking enough of me to describe me as a role model to his daughter. I saw that being *who I was*—a guy from the projects who had made it out and wanted to help other people—was more important than all the money and fame I thought I wanted, and this was why everything I have done in my whole life, good or bad, matters.

Whether you too have been unfocused or in need of discipline, gotten angry, been insecure, struggled with unhappiness, been unaccountable for your actions, misused power, or fought change—it all matters. It also matters how and if you have decided to address these negative behaviors, and how hard you've been willing to work toward changing them. How have you treated other people? Have you been compassionate? Hopeful? Loving?

In some small way, calling my sister set into action a whole series of events that had been going on for years, unknown to me. Action propels us forward on our journey when we take the first step toward change, and usually that step, whatever it is, is the most difficult one. But with that first step, you can connect fate to action, begin a new journey, and break down the mountain you erected for yourself long ago.

APPENDIX A: SHAOLIN STANCES

There is yin and yang in all things. You cannot do one thing without affecting the other, so if you take a journey to help heal your past and move forward in your future, it cannot be just a mental one. The mind and the body work as one, so to train the mind and neglect the body is to work against your ultimate purpose—which is to be happy and free from the trauma and difficulties of the past.

The following forms can help, by working your back, circulation, knees, and joints, and building strength at the same time. None of these forms are too advanced, so they are relatively easy to do on your own, but be warned, and be humble: much as I learned at the outset of my own Shaolin training, exercises that look easy are often deceptively complex because they work many different muscle groups at one time. Many times, you won't even realize how hard you're working until the next day, when you'll really feel it. It's also always best to have an experienced instructor around just to make sure you're doing it right, or to pick up another book where you can see the exact positions of the body through photographs and illustrations.

THE HORSE STANCE

This stance was named for the position you find yourself in at its deepest extension, which looks very much like how you would be sitting while riding a horse.

This stance works your core energy—the muscles in the entire body are being used, and getting stronger the longer you hold it.

For the horse stance, spread your legs a little more than shoulder width apart. Bend both knees slightly and then force the knees out to the sides. Very important, make sure that all your weight is centered. Don't bend forward even an inch, or you will defeat the whole purpose of the exercise. I have seen people do this and say their knees hurt. That is because they are leaning forward. You should feel the slight strain in the thighs and the glutes, not the back or the knees.

Once you are in the proper stance, put your hands together extended in front of you. You will notice that you can go lower and lower in the stance as you get stronger.

Next, slowly retract your hands, while breathing in slowly. Then, push the hands out slowly while exhaling. You should control the breathing so that when the hands have been fully extended you will have let all the air out.

You should repeat the process ten times before going to the next exercise. If after five you are not feeling enough strain in the proper areas, lower your stance. Once again, don't lean forward; keep the weight centered.

ELBOW-TO-TOE STRETCH

The most important stretch is the elbow to toe. It's called the "thousand-day" stretch. The masters say that if you do this exercise every day for one thousand days, you will be able to touch your chin to your toes.

With this exercise, you want to start with both legs together. Slowly bend your right knee; then take your left leg and place it at a forty-five-degree angle forward, locking it out (which means it's totally straight).

Next, slowly, from the waist down, with your right leg still bent and the left leg locked out straight, bend forward until you feel tightness in the left leg.

This next step is crucial: breathe. Most people hold their breath unconsciously, and this is not good. When you hold your breath, you slow down blood flow and oxygen circulation to your muscles and brain, which can lead to cramping.

You should hold this for a slow count of ten while regulating your breathing. Come back to position one, and repeat on the opposite side.

Doing both sides is considered to be one set: you should do three sets. The goal is to do three sets with a count of thirty on each leg.

SIDE-TO-SIDE STRETCH

This exercise will build strength in all parts of your legs and lower back while increasing flexibility.

Assume the position you did in the first exercise—the horse stance. This is a more difficult exercise to keep your back straight in. Fold your arms in front of you and straight out (so you can feel the strain in your shoulders). This is done to monitor whether your back is straight or not. If you see that you are dropping your arms, you are most likely bending forward.

Slowly bend the right leg. As your body shifts to the right, make your left leg straight and extended out to the side. Hold it there for a while.

Next, slowly shift your weight to the left, repeating the process for the other leg. It is very important, when shifting the weight from right to left, to make sure your weight is centered and your opposite leg is bent. If you straighten up, you will take the pressure off the legs, thus defeating the purpose of the exercise.

This should be repeated ten times. Shifting right to left once counts as one. You want to work up to fifty or more. The time you hold it depends on you. Start slowly, maybe for ten or twenty seconds each hold, and then work your way up to a minute each side.

SHAOLIN BREATHING AND BACK BENDING

This is the last exercise you will do in the set. Always end with this one. Breathing and back bending stretches everything: neck, back, glutes, and calves. It also induces rapid blood flow while developing your Chi, Chinese for "energy."

With your legs together and your hands interlocked in front of you, slowly move your hands up your body while inhaling and bending slightly back. By the time your hands are over your head and you are bending back, you should not be able to take in any more air.

Next, slowly bend forward all the way down while exhaling. It is very important that you exhale very slowly and not let all the air out until the exercise is complete. While still exhaling, grab the back of your legs and hold until you are completely out of breath.

Repeat.

If you are unable to grab your legs at first, work on the exercise without doing that part until you have developed enough flexibility to do so. Repeat this three more times. The goal is five. When you go down for the stretch, the idea is to touch your palms to the floor and then put your head between your legs.

You can accomplish many mind and body goals if you do these exercises each and every day, and they will provide you with renewed energy. You'll also greatly reduce the chance of illness if you work hard to exercise, maintain a proper diet, and train with more Shaolin exercises, which can be found in my martial arts book, *An American's Journey to the Shaolin Temple*.* You will feel great, and perform better in every way, which will affect how you deal with the rest of your life on a day-to-day basis.

---

*Steve DeMasco, *An American's Journey to the Shaolin Temple* (Black Belt Books, Ohara Publications, 2001).

APPENDIX B: WHAT ARE THE SHAOLIN FIVE ANIMAL FORMS?

These five animal forms are the basis for Shaolin, and though there are many different styles of the martial art and other animal forms are practiced in all of them, every Shaolin style relies on the basic Dragon, Tiger, Leopard, Snake, and Crane forms.

1. THE DRAGON

The dragon symbolizes grace, beauty, and great power. In Chinese mythology, the dragon evolved from water, so the form's movements are very fluid and circular. In the Dragon form, a Shaolin practitioner uses his or her hands like claws to grab and hold an opponent while delivering a powerful blow with another part of the body, or using his or her body to put weight on an opponent's joints. The power in the Dragon form comes from circular movements like twisting the body, and a focus on developing internal energy (Chi) to use against an opponent.

2. THE TIGER

The Chinese admire the tiger for its powerful claws and great strength and agility. Tiger training produces strong bones, joints, and tendons. Many of the Tiger form exercises are designed to strengthen the back and spine as well as the arms and forearms. The use of the hands in the tiger claw differs from the dragon claw because it will pull, rip, or tear at an opponent instead of holding him or her in place. The strength here comes from twisting the body and using the ground to execute powerful blows and kicks. The Tiger is the most physically challenging of the five animal forms, and practitioners also learn to mimic a tiger's real-life methods of stealth and attack, which the Chinese believe helps the practitioner anticipate an attacker's blows, and more powerfully deliver his or her own.

3. THE LEOPARD

The Chinese admire the leopard for its agility. The leopard is not as powerful as the tiger, but it is more agile. This form teaches a combination of speed and agile footwork to overcome opponents. The Leopard form uses both short and quick, powerful strikes to slowly confuse and defeat opponents. Short kicks are meant to hit the opponent's groin or abdomen, and the leopard form is a defensive and clever one. In life and in this form, the leopard uses subtle movements to move around an opponents' blows and is quick to strike. This elaborate footwork in the leopard form helps practitioners develop balance and timing.

4. THE SNAKE

The snake is admired for its ability to strike an aggressor quickly. Because a snake does not have legs, and must coil to strike with speed and power, the Snake form is all about speed. The Snake form has practitioners using their fingertips and palms to strike at an opponent's pressure points, and it is both offensive and defensive. Snake practitioners learn to generate powerful internal energy and release it in every blow. This means fighting from a relaxed state of mind, because doing so enables the fighter to go from waiting to making an offensive strike. The Snake form is the opposite of the Tiger form, using internal power rather than hard defensive blocks and blows.

5. THE CRANE

The Chinese like the crane's patience. It can hang out and stand on one leg for many hours without moving. This represents concentration and focus in Shaolin. The Crane form uses a hooking motion to fend off blows, divert the energy, and then strike from any distance. With its long wingspan and legs, cranes can put a lot of distance between themselves and an attacker, and so the Crane form involves sweeping kicks and mimicry of the bird's beak to strike quickly. The Crane form develops strong fingers, arms, and legs.

APPENDIX C: A DISCIPLINED MIND REQUIRES A HEALTHY BODY

The body is a temple filled with art. If you don't take care of the temple, there is no art.

In Shaolin, as you know, a strong mind and a strong body go together inseparably. By "strong," the Shaolin mean disciplined, and so they believe you cannot have a strong mind without also working hard to apply discipline to how you treat your body. That doesn't mean just doing exercises though, but also being disciplined enough to eat certain foods on a regular basis that your body needs to stay healthy and strong, and avoiding others at all costs. The physical discipline of actually doing exercise is why the monks do eight hours of kung fu every day. It gives them the focus to discipline themselves to meditate and pray, and in the typical yin-yang way we see pop up a lot in Shaolin, the meditation and prayer give them the discipline and strength to do those eight hours of kung fu.

In this country, many of us are undisciplined in our eating habits. Fast food is a way of life, and eating itself has become something we do in combination with other tasks, like having business meetings, going over office reports, or otherwise "multitasking." We try to make the most of our time, and we also seek to get something for nothing.

Part of the mythology surrounding healthy eating is founded on the very American notion of gluttony, as perpetuated by the diet industry, which encourages us to eat as many "low-fat" or "low-sugar" manufactured foods as we want. Most times, this results in chronic overeating. But by removing the fat content, or the processed sugar in diet foods, marketing is able to suggest that we can have as much as we want because there are fewer calories. No one mentions all the damage those excess chemicals (that make them able to say "fat-free" and "low-sugar") actually do.

As a middle-aged man who has been in the world of health and martial arts for over thirty years, I know that few of us like the idea of getting older, but of course it is inevitable, and if you don't take good care of yourself in specific ways that go beyond hitting the salad bar instead of fast food on a regular basis, or swearing off doughnuts every time you gain a pound or two, the aging process will be much more unpleasant.

Eastern cultures have known for aeons how integrally linked the mind, body, and spirit are; the prevailing wisdom about physical health in the West, however, has focused more on curing diseases with pills once we are already sick or weak physically, rather than coming at health from a more holistic and preventative place. We get shots to protect ourselves from getting sick, but most Western doctors don't prescribe exercise and healthy eating—they just give you pills after the fact.

Shaolin monks believe that each of us should live in balance, and that everything from exercise to eating should be moderated, which is probably why there aren't a whole lot of fat monks running around. You won't be surprised to hear that neither of these things fits very well into Western philosophy. You know how it goes: we want to be stronger, thinner, smarter, more attractive, or more muscled very fast, and we want to see results "yesterday." Looking at the American approach to exercise, Shaolin monks would probably just shake their heads and wonder what we're trying to accomplish.

THE YO-YO PHENOMENON

With our high and often unrealistic expectations, most of us will never be happy with the results of our fitness or diet programs, which explains the phenomenon of "yo-yo" dieting, where we're constantly on and off diets to moderate our weight, rather than eating in a consistently healthy way and having the discipline to do the exercise needed to maintain cardiovascular fitness and a weight appropriate for our frame.

It has been statistically proven that most people who lose weight on a diet gain it back, largely because many diets limit the types of foods you can eat. Thus, you are forced to eat more of the same food groups instead of keeping your daily intake diverse enough to include meats (protein), fruits, vegetables, and whole grains. For example, the very popular low-carbohydrate, high-protein diet of the past few years is challenging for those who try to go back to "normal" eating after they feel they have shed enough weight.

This diet has become so popular because many people

have lost so much weight on it, much more than on most other diets. However, after a while, eating all protein gets boring. How many ham-and-cheese omelets can you swallow? Soon you feel yourself groping like a criminal for the leftover mashed potatoes in the fridge in the middle of the night.

EATING FOR LIFE

The Chinese have a different philosophy about the aging process, which does not go well with what every single fashion and fitness magazine tells us here in the West. In the East, when you get older, you get wiser, and the Chinese think you should focus on trying to age well until you die, not pretend that you're not getting older or that you'll never die. They prepare themselves as soon as they can, so that when they get to be thirty, forty, fifty years old and more, they are way ahead of the game.

It would be hard to eat like a Shaolin monk though, unless you have a particular affinity for tofu, plain rice, and bok choi. They maintain a strict Buddhist vegan diet, which means that they will not eat meat or anything that is a derivative of meat, like eggs. When I returned from my first visit to China to meet the abbot, I tried this way of eating. The tofu's not bad, by the way: it can be prepared to taste like chicken and steak, which has amazed me no end, and it tastes great; this is one of the things I look forward to each year when I go to train at the Shaolin temple.

Foods like these are so natural and easy for your body to process that once you get into a rhythm of eating them, they generally cease to seem weird or bad. When the primary function of food is sustenance over taste, it ceases to have the social value many cultures attach to the family meal and eating.

The Shaolin Buddhist diet contains far too many carbohydrates for the average person, who might spend eight hours a day in an office chair, on the phone, and one or two hours a day on his or her feet walking home, cooking dinner, or picking up the kids. In spite of the sameness and limitations of the Shaolin monks' diet, many people would gain weight on what appears to be a very spartan existence because unlike them, you're not training for close to eight hours a day.

So what is good, given all the "bad" foods we're constantly warned to stay away from? There are a few factors we have to consider that are inherent in our lifestyle, most of which cannot be avoided. If you eat store-bought food, as you probably know, you are being served many hormones and chemicals. Unless we eat all organically grown fruits, vegetables, and meats, this can't be avoided.

If you can't maintain a totally organic diet, you might start more realistically by monitoring your carbohydrate intake. Instead of eating toast or cereal for breakfast, I often start out with a protein shake. After much research on these products— and that includes tasting some pretty vile concoctions—I've realized that there are some very good high-protein, low-carbohydrate shakes on the market. Most of them also have low sugar levels.

Sugar is considered by nutritionists everywhere to be a "bad" food. Another hidden source of the stuff is alcohol, which also contains a lot of carbohydrates, as do fruit juices. Generally speaking, fruit itself is healthy to eat, as fruits contain a lot of water *and* vitamins, but the juice derivatives are far too concentrated and your system immediately turns the sugar in them to fat. In the fruit family, melons, apples, and berries are the best. I would suggest not eating fruit mixed with protein, and having the fruit alone as a snack.

It's difficult for our bodies to absorb protein, so many nutritionists have maintained that we need to take in a lot more of it than what is required. Protein is the only thing we take in that retains muscle.

Every carbohydrate you put into your mouth turns to sugar; if you're trying to avoid the eventual fat this creates, you can intersperse at least two protein shakes during the day with a very low carbohydrate diet, which might include just one slice of bread and a salad with protein like chicken, tuna, or red meat.

Meal skipping is a problem for many people in this culture: we reason that we are often too busy to eat. Work, children, or social obligations are all excuses frequently given by those who don't eat a balanced diet. Try not to do this. Your body is constantly working, like an energized wheel that just keeps going. If you don't eat, the wheel stops, then starts again. All it takes is small snacks throughout the day to keep that wheel moving, and keep you in a better frame of mind. Eating like a bird is usually best—which means four or five little snacks throughout the day, like vegetables or shakes, so that you stay on track.

STEVE'S DIET

Just so you get an idea of what a healthy diet is (or a diet healthier than your current one), I've included a sample of what I typically eat three times a day:

Morning
- Protein shake, with soy milk (you can use low-fat milk) and at least 30 grams of protein. I myself do about 50 grams.
- Kung fu training for a couple of hours, followed by more training with students.

- After my workout I will have another shake, with the same amount of protein. This time I use water to mix with the protein powder.

- About two hours later I eat an apple because it's better to eat smaller amounts but continually throughout the day, so your body is constantly working that treadmill.

BREAKFAST can be a couple of eggs if you want with a little fruit. I still don't like mixing fruit with meals. It slows down the digestive process. When I eat eggs for breakfast, I like to scramble two eggs, with two or three more egg whites with it. Two egg yolks is more than enough. I will also mix some fresh spinach or kale in with my eggs. Sometimes in the late morning, after my workout, I will have a cup of coffee. I don't have coffee with breakfast; it also slows down the digestive process. I have never seen a Shaolin monk at the temple drinking coffee, since they generally frown upon stimulants; however, one of my kung fu masters told me I could never be a master if I didn't drink coffee. He loved coffee, and was an excellent grand master, so I couldn't argue with him.

Afternoon

- Salad with meat in it for lunch. Or tuna on low-carb wheat bread.

- Two hours later I eat another apple.

Evening

- Chicken, fish, veal, lean pork, or a small amount of steak for dinner. I personally don't like to eat steak at night; it's difficult to digest, and I wake up in the middle of the night with bad dreams when I do eat it.

- With dinner I will have a green vegetable like spinach, broccoli, or green beans. My kids will have rice or potatoes or pasta, in addition to all of the above. I don't. The only carbohydrate I will eat at dinner is the vegetable. My children are physically very active and can use and handle the pasta or rice, but on me it will only go to waste, and eventually, the dreaded "tire."

- That's it for the night. *No dessert!*

THE "COOKIE MONSTER" IS EATING YOUR KIDS

Kids are a whole different story. It is hard for everyone to stay away from sugar and processed carbohydrates, but especially so for children, when the media promotes cookies, cakes, and breads, the store shelves are fully stocked with them, and most everyone around them eats like crap as well.

Keeping your children on low-carbohydrate, low-sugar diets is far easier if they are raised this way—rather than noticing that your child has started to become "chubby" toward adolescence. When I was a chief instructor in Concord, New

Hampshire, many years ago, I would always ask my students, "What did you have for breakfast and lunch today?" Inevitably, they would answer that they had had some sort of sugar cereal for breakfast, and for lunch a peanut butter and "marshmallow fluff" sandwich or a granola bar, which is usually all sugar.

Forgetting how easily influenced children are by adults they look up to, I once said in jest that the sugar would make their brains go soft and that they should all eat pasta for breakfast instead. Well the first time I said that, and the last, was when about 99 percent of the kids' parents told me that their children came home that night and told them they must eat pasta for breakfast, not cereal.

Well, even though pasta wasn't the best breakfast for them, it was surely better than sugar cereal. From that day on, I started giving my students responsible nutritional instruction in a serious way.

My three sons have always eaten organic eggs, toast, whole milk, and fruit for breakfast. However, as kids do, they still like to have pancakes with blueberries in them every once in a while. Even though we make them with unbleached flour, whole milk, and eggs, *our* pancakes aren't good for the boys either. Still, in life and in diet one has to compromise sometimes, and my wife and I rationalize that pancakes like this are better than Eggo waffles, some sort of pop-in microwave meal, or a sugar cereal.

There have been countless reports on the effects of sugar on the body, especially for children, whose hyperactivity is often diagnosed by medical doctors and managed with drugs like Ritalin. If you want to experiment with the ways in which sugar negatively affects your kids, try taking them off sweets and reducing their carbohydrates for two days, then watch for the difference in their behavior. Many of my students have been diagnosed with attention deficit disorder or attention deficit/hyperactivity disorder; after taking them off of sugar, there were tremendous positive results, which included the kids becoming calmer and more able to focus on chores and homework.

Children's systems are far more sensitive to vitamins, minerals, and dietary elements than adults' systems, so when these diets are initiated, they must be done with extreme care, and generally, the higher-protein-providing foods need to be integrated slowly. One way to begin to elevate your kids' protein intake is through one of the shakes I mentioned earlier, which feature low sugar and low carbohydrates.

Sometimes you have to camouflage the healthy elements of a child's diet. In the morning, tell the children you are making them a milk shake for breakfast—a special treat. Don't start them with a shake that has more than 24 grams of protein in the beginning, and be on the lookout for their complaints of stomachaches or other gastrointestinal pain. As adults, we can handle shakes containing up to 50 grams two or three times a day, but children's constitutions are obviously more delicate.

APPENDIX D:
CHINESE TRADITIONAL TEA CEREMONY FOR LONGEVITY, HAPPINESS, AND GOOD FORTUNE

The Chinese have long believed that tea, prepared and drunk the right way, can hold the keys to your future. The drinking of Chinese tea prepared this way, where the water for the tea is boiled in a stainless-steel pot, is part of a traditional tea ceremony that if done right is said to help bring forth good things for the drinker.

What you will need (serving items come with traditional Chinese tea set):

Hot water

Tea leaves

Traditional teapot

Stainless-steel teapot

Smelling cup

1. Warm up the entire tea set with hot water, then empty.

2. Put tea leaves into the traditional teapot.

3. Pour hot water into a stainless steel teapot.

4. Pour water out of the stainless steel teapot and into the traditional teapot (washing tea leaves).

5. Pour hot water into the traditional teapot from the stainless steel teapot again (wait about two minutes).

6. Pour tea into the big jug (comes with traditional Chinese tea set) and pour tea into the smelling cup (also included in set).

7. Put tasting cup (short one) on the top of the smelling cup (longer one) and turn them over with one hand. Take the smelling cup up and move it around the tasting cup three times for collecting tea flavor, then smell it.

8. Put the smelling cup to the left of the tea saucer. With three fingers, hold the tasting cup and finish the tea with three sips.

The three sips are for:

1. Longevity

2. Happiness

3. Good Fortune